Workplace

Unwritten Policies

Academic vs Experiential Views

Volume 1: Basic Organizational Structure

40 Years of Working Experience,

7 industries,

29 Organizations,

Worldwide.

By James Ostad

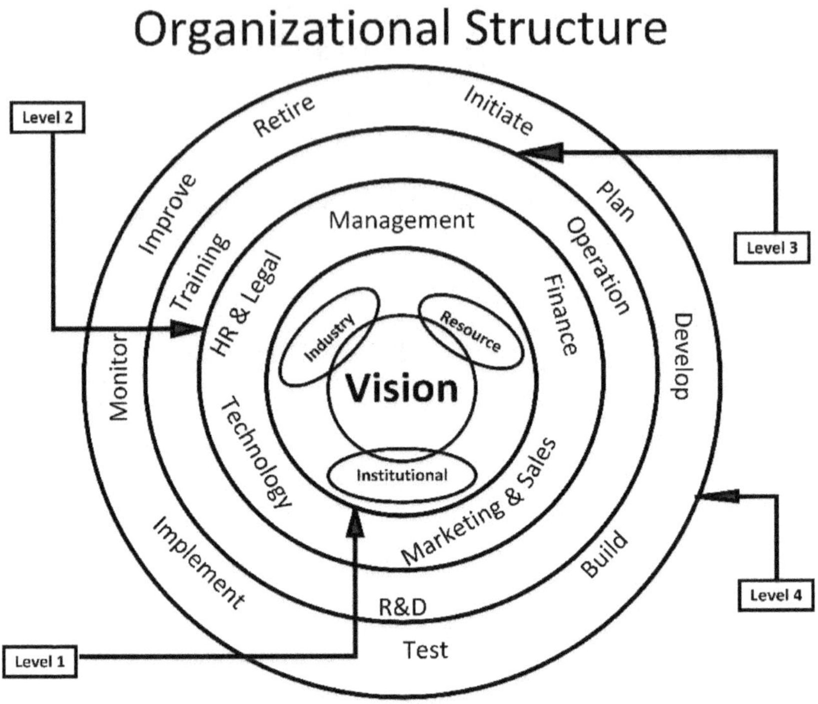

Figure 1 Organizational Structure

Figure 1 Description: A vision is an idea within an industry, and with the consideration of the institutional requirements, that would need resources to form an organizational structure, to bring that vision to reality, and deliver it to a consumer.

Copyright © 2026

First edition: 2026

Volume 1: Basic Organizational Structure

Publisher: BSGE L.L.C.

James Ostad

Published in the United States of America

First Publication: 2026

Paperback ISBN- 978-1-7352059-2-2

Disclaimer:

No existing company or organization will be used in the content of this book's volumes; only in the reference section, showing where the author worked. All contents and cases are the author's experiences at those workplaces. This is not an instructional manual; thus, it is the reader's choice to use any of the case studies in their own workplace practices.

No part of this book has been created by any "AI content creator."

Dedication

To my wife, Karen, my mother, my oma, who always encouraged me in my work and study.

Table of Contents

Epigraph

"One cannot learn how to swim without being in the water."

You will not be afraid of water if you understand and respect its nature.

Preface

It is human nature to explore, to innovate, and to change. By doing so, we try to learn from our past and get better.

At age 14, I thought I knew it all, and I did not need any guidance, an attitude of "I can do it by myself". That was when I learned my first lesson in honesty and integrity. I was working at a carpentry shop as an apprentice. The first mistake was stealing from my boss. The second mistake was lying about it. I paid the price for that and learned a lesson. Do not lie or steal. I learned one more thing as a side effect of that event: courage. It takes courage to be honest and have integrity at work. With that, you will earn a lifetime of respect.

Understanding why, what, when, where, and who (5 Ws), and, of course, how the changes and events happen in our lives will set the stage for your working career. Learning the answers to those questions would be faster if you have an instructional book at hand. Not everyone has a role model at home who helps them in life. Not everyone has a mentor at work who would genuinely care about their success. Learning is like boiling water; if you turn off the heat, it will cool. Initiating a learning strategy for life is up to you.

The title of this book references all kinds of workplaces, from a small shop to a large factory complex assembly line, or a small business office to a global corporation.

The uniqueness of this book lies in sharing workplace experiences from 29 organizations in 7 industries across the global space where the author worked, a summation of 40 years of working experience. At the same time, it must be recognized that academic education and professional training have tremendous value in recognizing events, analyzing their attributes, and finally summarizing the results of those events, along with their impacts on the economy, employees, and society as a whole.

Without an educational foundation, this book would not have been possible.

A learning from Dale Carnegie Course: “Before talking about a subject matter, present to the audience that you have the qualifications on the subject matter.”

By combining education and experience, you can see the value of a book.

The purpose of this is not just to depict the changes and events, but to present an analytical explanation of those events so that you can use it as a benchmark at your workplace, to compare the changes and events. That would be insider information for you to use at your workplace.

Learning and understanding the usage of the major industry standard processes and procedures, such as ITIL, Six-Sigma, or TQM (see reference section for further details), will help you to organize your career and plan ahead for some major organizational changes and events that would impact your career.)

Everyone is destined to make mistakes at some point in their lives. The best one could do is to learn from the past, plan at the present, and be ready for the future.

By reading this book series, you will capture some of the most common changes and events in a workplace, and figure out what strategy you would plan for yourself when a similar change or event happens.

How would you know if your company is going to be bankrupt? What would you do to save your career? Could you prepare yourself for such events?

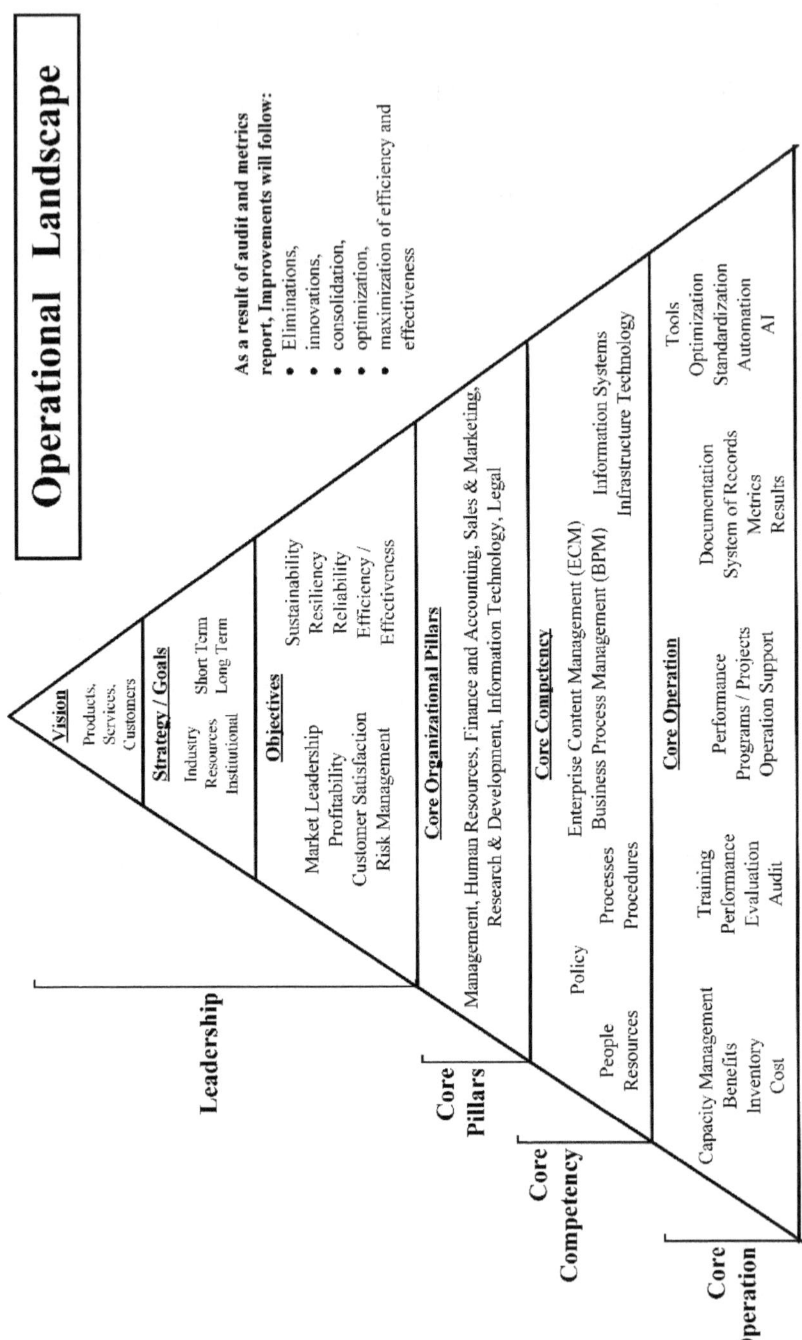

Figure 2 - Organizational Landscape

Figure 2 Description: Regardless of the industry, any organization must have a vision to start with. Under the vision, products and services would be created and delivered to the targeted customers. The goals and strategy will provide the foundation for the rest. It will focus on a specific industry and gather the needed resources to plan for short- and long-term goals and strategy, in alignment with institutional guidelines, laws, and regulations. The objectives will define the character of its behavior on which it operates.

The structure of an organization includes hierarchical pillars within its functions. Each pillar would have a set of core competencies to operate under, to achieve its expected performance and targeted results. In the big picture of operation, all designated pillars will work together in a seamless, coherent, and transparent landscape.

Learning about the company structure should be one of your goals, as it will help you to gain a perspective on the big picture, inside and out, in any industry.

There is a handful of branches in an organization that shape the structure:

- Leadership and management, Human Resources (HR), Finance and Accounting, Sales, Marketing, Legal, Research & Development (R&D), and Information Systems / Infrastructure Technology (IS/IT).

These core pillars exist in every organization. You might see them under different names or as a combined one, yet the functionality of each pillar would always remain the same.

A major change that affects not only employees but also the community is a mass layoff. Several organizational strategies and behaviors are involved in this single event, which will be discussed in this book and will shape the book's core value.

The takeaway would be:

- There will always be a change, an event that will impact your job and employment.
- There are some strategies for the workforce to be able to manage any change to survive its impacts and risks.

After learning about the structure, understanding a company's operations becomes the next goal. It is through the operational settings that you can better recognize changes or events and their impacts on you and your workplace.

In this book volume, the major pillars of any organization will be reviewed at a high level. The second volume of this book is based on captured experiences across multiple companies, from small to global businesses, in 7 different industries. As part of a case study of a company transformation, change, or event, and its impact on its workforce, a case will include the following sections:

1. The transformation **introduction**.
2. An **academic** overview of the transformation.
3. The **reality** check of the transformation, what was **experienced**.
4. A **benchmark** between the academic and the experiential views.
5. An **analytical evaluation** to extract the best practices and the worst practices of the transformation, with its **impact** on the workforce.
6. The **summary** of the case, with its lesson learned.

The third volume will provide a summary of this book series, from leadership to operations. It will offer strategies for employees to consider in their planning and preparation to manage major organizational changes and events, such as mass layoffs.

By the time you are done with the first volume of this book, you will have a perspective when next time you encounter a company's transformation, having a thought about the following questions:

- What is the Organizational Operation?
- Who are the key stakeholders to uphold an operational performance?
- What is Operational Excellence, the definition, and the practical views?

- How do you frame an Operational Excellence, in relation to its change or transformation, to better understand its cause and effect?
- Did we get the change result we expected to get, as was planned, during the initial setup of the strategy and goals?
- Finally, how would this change affect me, my job, and my career

You will gain a perspective of what "Operational Excellence" looks like, or what the definition of it is, or what evidence should be there to prove that. The term applies not only to the IS/IT department pillar, but to all pillars; they are connected and feed each other in a 360-degree loop.

The uniqueness of the industries in which this author has worked is that they all have an IS/IT department. They all use technology to do their daily operational work.

Why should you read this book?

How ready are you if your manager tells you, "Thank you for your service, your work is no longer needed with this company"?

The content of this book is a summation of over 40 years of working experience:

- Hired, fired, quit, laid off,
- Bankruptcies,

- JV (joint venture),
- Merger & Acquisition (M&A),
- Closure (end of the business),
- Split-Up (demerger or spin-off),
- and a new start-up.

The educational degrees, professional certifications, and countless organizational trainings are all key elements for putting this book's content together.

You could be part of any of the main pillars of the organization: Leadership, Management, Finance, Human Resources, Information Technology, Legal, Research and Development, or Sales and Marketing.

"Knowledge is power."

Introduction

There are three volumes in this book's edition. The first volume will provide a high-level overview of an organizational operation to illustrate a roadmap for the reader, so anyone can gain a perspective on the big picture and what a structure would look like, without having any formal management education, as they read the rest of the volumes. The structure will include the strategic and tactical aspects.

Once the big picture is introduced, volume two will introduce the core purpose: an analytical evaluation of each event or change.

Those events and changes were real workplace changes that had a long-lasting impact on the author's working career and on other working-class employees.

As a reader, you would be able to see the evolution of organizational behavior, especially in its management and Human Resources pillars, through real-time practices rather than through written strategy or policy. This is the key element of this book, providing an unwritten policy, rather than textbook content.

Note: A written policy and strategy do not dictate its actual practices, as you will read in every case study in this series. The intention here is not to be just another instructional content or a textbook.

Finally, the 3rd volume of this book edition would summarize the first two volumes into 3 sections:

a) What are the major events that would harm the working class?
b) What are some strategies that the working class could use to protect themselves and minimize the impact of those changes or events?
c) Finally, an outline of what worked the best, and what did not work, the strategies that would benefit any employee at any workplace in any industry.

To give a sample of what to expect from a case study, here is a real event from the past.

Note: no specific year, location, company name, or individual name would be given in any of the case studies. This is to prevent any privacy violation, any reputational defamation, or business disparagement. At the same time, the case studies in this book are all based on true events.

Sample case study

Under company policy, an employee at a small electronic factory is entitled to 1 week of paid time off after 1 full year of employment. On the day of one of the employee's full-year completions, the owner of the factory handed him his weekly paycheck and, with a cheering smile, told him," John, I have to let you go because I do not want to give you a week's paid vacation."

That employee had no idea what to say or do, took the check, and left the shop. He sat in his car for a while, thinking about his rent, car loan payment, and all other expenses. Living on his own was not an easy pill to swallow. All he was thinking at that age was what he should do next. He just wanted to get back to work and pay his bills to survive. With no experience in such events, he had no other thought about why he was fired. He already had a goal of leaving factory work and getting an education. But he was not ready yet. (Note: this is a principal factor for any working-class employee, emphasizing a skill set for further employment, either trade training, such as a plumber, or a college-level study.

After decades, he thought about what had happened. The owner of that shop let him go because the business had been slowing down for months. He did not want to warn anyone about the factory's final days, so no one would quit before the last production line was finished. He was thinking about his business and security, as well as his retirement. Everyone else was just a resource to be used and worked until the last day.

The employees were so busy with their work and life that they did not think about what happened at that time. Back to John: since he did not consider the obvious triggers, causes, and effects, he learned nothing about that event. He did not have any education, any professional training, or any experience to be able to see ahead of the change or event, so that he could protect himself ahead of that day, the sudden let-go day.

- Could he have done something to secure his exit before his forced exit day?
- Were there any triggers and signs that he could have recognized as a sign of trouble down the road for the factory?
- What could he have done to secure his exit?

A business must survive. For that reason, there will always be changes and events. That is only one variable that is not in your control, the business vision and goal, as well as its strategy. You could impact the goal and strategy, but only the leadership could decide on a change.

But there are many variables you can control. The biggest challenge for people like John is managing his career and making the right choices. He needed to build a skill set that would have helped him navigate his career through any job market. As part of that skill set, it was to understand the operations, the so-called "Corporate Plan or Strategy."

"Learning and education take time and require sacrifices to achieve and obtain key skill sets."

Not everyone is made to become an engineer, a lawyer, or a doctor. At the same time, not every job is asking you to have a college degree or a certificate. Yet, there is a common characteristic among all of us, curiosity, for some more than others. That is when John should have noticed that his workload was decreasing each day. A simple calculation would have been: "If I am not building anything, there would not be any revenue for the company to pay my paycheck, therefore, I will be out of a job soon."

Time is changing fast. Back in the day, one could have had a job as a Software Developer before even obtaining a college degree. But now, for the very same job, the hiring managers are asking for some degree, skills, or experience. The sense of giving someone a chance to get started at the bottom does not come easily. You will read about this type of opportunity in a case involving extreme favoritism in which a group of managers practices its own unwritten policy, to the point of harming the organizational productivity and cost, to keep and hire unskilled and uneducated family members or close friends. We will revisit this in volume two, among other cases.

In the above example, if John had any skills, certificates, or educational degrees, he would have had more options to pursue another job. That does not mean he would have had an easier route.

- Could John have seen the end of the tunnel, gotten a layoff notice, or been laid off, if he had noticed the operational slowdown?
- Could John have had better visibility if he had learned more about the factory's operational structure?

John was so busy with his work and day-to-day survival that he never got a chance to focus on what caused the slowdown and what its effects might have been. Let us assume that John saw what was coming: the factory closure. What do you think he should have done:

- Quit, and find another job?
- Stay to the end, either being let go or till the last day of the factory?

Either of the above options has its own risks and impacts on the working class. You will read about cases for each of the above options, providing strategy, pros and cons, results, long-term impact, or success, etc., which you could use for your own career path decision.

To emphasize the above case, let us look at another sample case with a far broader impact, with a company with thousands of employees.

Decades ago, in a large corporation, a newly appointed CIO opened a town hall session to introduce a major enterprise program to build a new data center. As part of his speech, he said: “There will be about 340+ new jobs by the time we complete the new building.”

Well, by the time the new endeavor was built and fully operational, the employees received their pink slips with boxes, and mass layoffs followed.

The real-time triggers and events are more evidence than what a CIO would say or present. The employees need to be more attentive to the events and changes than what they are being told or shown. This is not about whether the leadership tells lies or the truth. It is about paying attention and planning for your future to secure your employment and career. Not every job change is due to a problem within the existing organization. You might decide to change your career for a better job. Some engineers are taxi drivers, or taxi drivers who became doctors.

With close attention to operations, you could see what would come long before it happened. Moreover, you could prepare yourself for that type of event as well, i.e., mass layoffs. There are hard choices to make for being ready for such events that are in your control; one would be to pay off your mortgage as fast as you can. That is one of the biggest challenges for a working-class family to survive after a mass layoff, among other challenges.

A critical thinking to be explored:

- What could you do to protect yourself and be prepared for such workplace events?

This is only one aspect of the contents here. There are several attributes to discuss for each event or change in an organization, and what you can do to be in a safe place to survive. Nothing in here is random. Any content here has a reason and fully grounded evidence to show its value.

"Maslow's hierarchy of needs" is a great template to keep close by, as a reminder of where you stand today in that pyramid.
(https://en.wikipedia.org/wiki/Maslow's_hierarchy_of_needs)

When the author was first introduced to this concept, he did not grasp its meaning beyond its shape. It really took him about a decade or so to finally understand its meaning and how it could help him navigate his life in general, including his career.

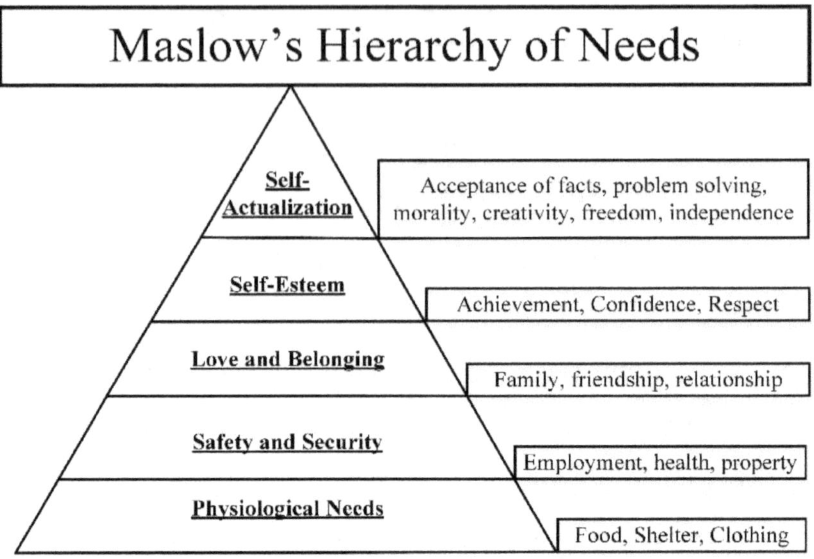

Figure 3 - Maslow's Hierarchy

It is strongly recommended to everyone to at least browse the concept, see what you understand from it, and do a surface-level comparison of your own life and career with this pyramid. Once you review its meanings at each level, then ask yourself:

- Do you think you have what you need in your life?
- Are you safe and secure?
- Are you satisfied and confident?

Only you could make that assessment.

To reiterate the purpose of this book, the intent is not about a company or an individual leader or a manager, but the events and the behaviors of those entities will be examined through a carefully structured framework to provide a mix of science-based and experience-based workbook for the working class to have as a toolbox at hand at the time of trouble.

By utilizing the best practices and strategies currently practiced in today's industries, when an event or a change, such as mass layoffs, happens, many employees would start asking questions like:

- What is happening?
- How did this happen?
- Why did this happen?
- How would this change impact my job and employment?
- When would I be impacted?
- What are we going to do next?

For many who have never experienced mass layoffs, such events might be devastating, as they were for many people during the 2000-2 financial downturn.

For some who had prior experience, it was still a challenging time, yet they had lessons from the past to guide them. In 2007-8, the collapse of the housing market and its mortgage industry caused a recession, with many people losing their jobs, homes, and savings. One category of people who were not affected as much as others were those who paid off their mortgages sooner than the loan term, by sacrificing their comfort and spending habits.

For some people, a small percentage, move to the next chapter of their lives, retirement, or find a hobby to pursue for a while, or a part-time job till retirement. Even within this group, the choice to do so will not be easy.

Decades ago, having a work pension was attainable, and a 401 (k) was just another option. With a pension, there was a safety net, a sense of security at work. It also added a sense of loyalty to the organization.

Now, in the year 2025, there are not only very few companies offering pensions, but also, among those that do, a strategy in place to take away those pensions through a systematic process implemented by leadership/management and Human Resources. You will read further in the following sections and chapters of those strategies; some happened decades ago, and some happened in very recent years.

As for the 401 (k) option, it has evolved. The fund is currently managed by a third party, which collects a substantial fee. The 401 (k) case study has its own discussion beyond this book.

Reminder: you always have a choice to make: invest in a 401(k) or another retirement investment, or put your money into assets, such as a house, to pay your mortgage sooner rather than later.

Why is it critical to understand your organizational operation? By understanding your employer's operation, you can better plan your employment and career. You could plan for your retirement and future employment, knowing ahead of time whether the organization would change direction, which would affect your employment.

Through his 40 years of experience, the author learned that employment is a two-way street. The employer has an option to terminate him, and he also has an option to move to another employer. But unfortunately, the employers will always have an advantage over him. The only way that advantage could be leveled is through his right decision-making for his own career.

The decision is yours, and if your employer is smart and values your work and experience, then that organization will work hard to keep you employed.

You will read an amazing career journey to find out:

- Why would you want to leave the company?
- Why would you want to stay with a company despite a toxic environment?
- How could you make yourself a valuable employee?

- What is more important: expertise, loyalty, connection, etc.?
- How would an organization see your values?
- What is your manager's role in your employment?
- What is HRM's role in your employment?

By understanding the above factors in your career path, you will be closer to being actualized on top of Maslow's hierarchy of needs. That is your moment to be so strong and experienced that not even the latest management and HR strategy and tactical elements in their hands would be able to harm your career.

If you ever get to that point, you will experience great satisfaction, a surreal moment, and the accomplishment of your life. This is the intent of this book: to get you closer to the top of the pyramid by providing you with a toolkit of actionable strategies in the workplace so that you can benefit from it.

At the same time, the leadership and management, as well as Human Resource pillars, would see how the new workforce is being equipped, so that they would manage their organization for the common good, a win-win situation for all.

While reading this book, you would want to think about the following major questions:

a) What could you do to **minimize** an event or a change in your employment? i.e., obtain a robust skill set, or study your employer's structure.
b) What are some **signs or triggers** that would indicate a coming change, such as mass layoffs? We are talking about any events or changes that could negatively impact your employment. i.e., an enterprise program suddenly ends.
c) How to **identify the behavior** of an event, such as a mass layoff? Note: HR has adopted a systematic approach to manage public relations and mitigate any negative reputational impact resulting from the mass layoff. Some of the cases here will illustrate the latest actions and strategies by the HR pillar. i.e., a new program starts, involving only a select group of employees, rather than the skilled ones with expertise.
d) What or how to **respond** to a change, or an event like a mass layoff at your organization? Or any HR strategy? (This is the heart of this book's content, yet to come.)

Basic

Organizational Structure

Chapter 1: The Overall Review

This chapter intends to provide a basic understanding of an organizational structure, regardless of its size, industry, or geographical location.

To understand the nature of a workplace, one needs to be familiar with the dynamics and interconnectedness. By understanding the employer's nature, one would have a better grasp of the workplace nature and how to navigate and perform.

Before a business exists, there must be an individual or group who initiates a vision to provide a product or service, and then it is created.

For a small business, that individual would be the CEO or president, to start with. We will talk about the vision later, but for now, that person starts it all. Let us understand or get a perspective on who the CEO is.

The idea of having an organization, a community, and a group of people started in a cave.

The chief cave dweller must address the following for the cave people so that they would want to stay:

a. Food

b. Shelter (safety and security)

c. Clothing

Ever since, people with ideas and visions have attracted others to join them and form an organization. Any place of work would have and need the following common features:

1. There are two types of organizational asset categories:
    a. Product (a tangible item for sale, i.e., cars, shoes, clothes, etc.)
    b. Services (intangible items: legal advice, teaching, doctor treatment, police services, etc.)
        i. Note: an organization could have either category or both.
2. There are two types of work: manual and intellectual, considering the division of work.
    a. Manual: construction workers, assembly line workers, plumbers, electricians, etc.
    b. Intellectual: teachers, lawyers, doctors, engineers, etc.
        i. Note: A worker could provide both types of work.
3. A group of people works toward a common goal. They would provide a mix of assets and work to help sell their products and services to target customers, generating revenue.
4. There must be a source of funds, material, money, earnings, etc., so that there would be compensation for those who work for that organization.
5. A targeted market, geographical location, with a willing customer to buy those products and services. After all, without customers, there will be no sales and, therefore,

no revenue, leading to bankruptcy. Hold on to this thought, as it will come back again.

Like the chief cave dweller, a CEO must do the same. Now, due to progress, the CEO will not provide food, shelter, or clothing directly; instead, they will provide monetary compensation so the working class can obtain their own food, shelter, and clothing.

Someone would need to initiate a vision for an organization to exist, called a leader, a visionary, or a CEO. A visionary, a leader, or a CEO would investigate the marketplace to identify the demands and needs customers want to pay for, and then initiate the creation of the products or services that can be made. Then the CEO would need people to create those products and services so customers would buy them. In return for the work in producing the products and services, the organization would compensate the workforce. Those products and services would be sold to raise money to cover its operating costs, including its workforce.

The following illustration illustrates the simplest concept among four entities with intertwined dependencies. What does this mean exactly?

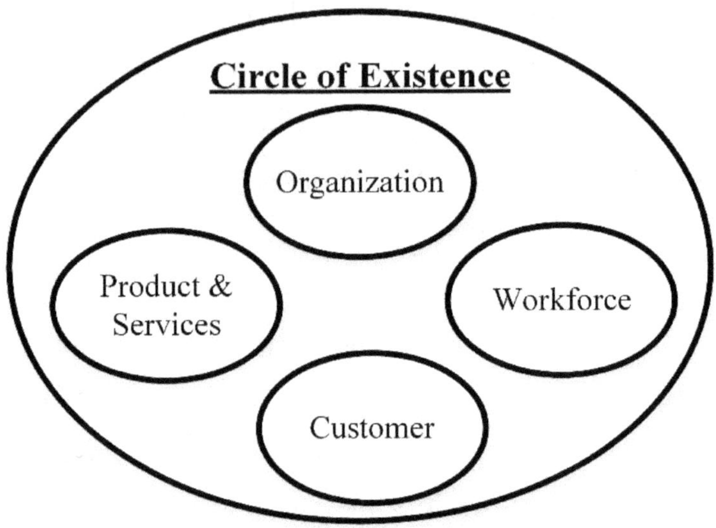

Figure 4 - Circle of Existence (a)

In a simple sentence, if you remove any of the following entities from the circle, the circle will not exist. For example, if there are no customers, why would a business build or create anything? If there are no products or services, what would it sell to a customer? If there is no workforce, how would it create the products and services for sale? If there is no organization, then that is clear; other elements would not exist.

You might say, how about a self-employed person? Well, you are right. Please note that this book addresses a structure, not a single small business such as a tailor, plumber, electrician, or shoemaker.

This network of dependencies must be maintained carefully to ensure a sustainable operation.

Think about this:

- If the workforce is not compensated accordingly, they will go somewhere else.
- If the customer is not happy with the product or service, they will go somewhere else.
- If a CEO is not seeing a sustainable operation, the CEO will close the door for the business. (This is only one scenario out of many that would happen.)

Let us look at the creation of a small business.

Once upon a time, there was a tailor family. The norm was that when a boy reached 7, he should start working as an apprentice. Well, one of the boys did so. By the time he was 22, he opened his tailoring shop with 18 workers.

As time passed and he got older, he transitioned his strategy to add pre-made clothes to his shop for sale, creating a clothing store. Later, he was selling only pre-made clothes, with no workers left to work for him. He got old and changed his business strategy. He did not plan to put the 18 workers out of business, but the changes in society and the economy forced him to do so to survive.

Let us add one more entity to the circle of existence, the work compensation.

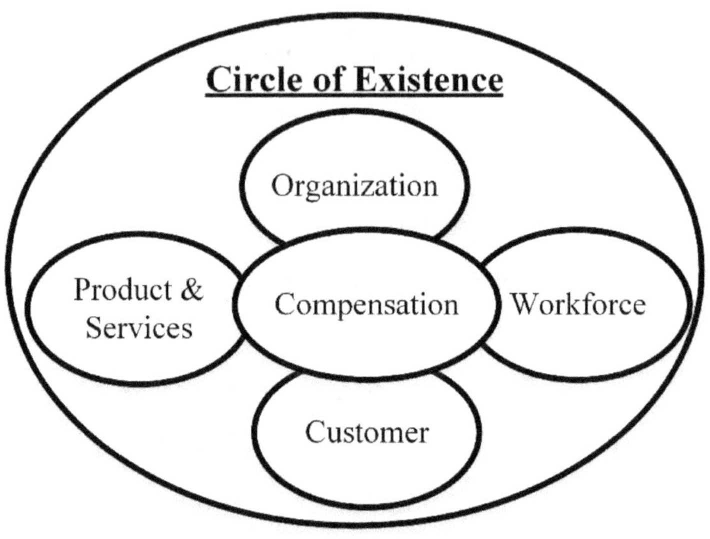

Figure 5 - Circle of Existence (b)

Just like an organization today, if a company cannot keep up with changes in society and the broader economy, it will collapse.

There is an existential balance among the five entities now. You see that the compensation overlaps with that of all other entities. This single entity is a multi-dimensional variable. The nature and values of each of the other entities differ.

Business compensation is like workforce compensation, the benefit of continuing the business.

Compensation for products and services would translate into the quality of those products and services, ensuring they are sustainable and reliable. Two effective strategies used by some organizations are adopting industry standards, such as Six Sigma and ITEL, and emphasizing strong audits, such as the Malcolm Baldrige Performance Excellence.

Keep this concept in mind as you further read the coming chapters and sections. It is vital to understand this concept, as it will help you better navigate changes and events during its operation.

Up to this point, what you just read was a basic illustration of an organizational structure. Now, let us step into each unit or pillar.

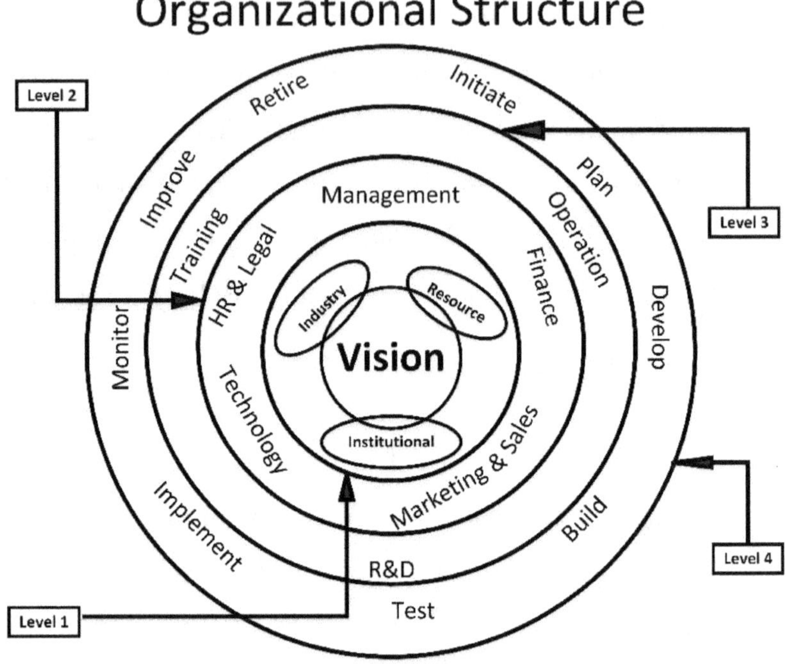

Figure 6 - Organizational Structure

To operate, it needs a basic structure, a business charter, a governing team, or a business plan.

At any given business, there must exist three basic functionalities or levels that would start an operation in a society and economy, considering its vision:

1. Industry: what is the focus of the products and services, i.e., bank, retail, manufacturing
2. Resources: who is the workforce, and what skill set levels do they have

3. Institutional: the laws and regulations with which the operation must comply.

At the core, an organization has the following pillars:

- Leadership and management
- Finance and Accounting
- Human Resources Management (HRM)
- Sales and Marketing (S&M)
- Research and Development (R&D)
- Information Technology (IT)
- Legal

There are four levels of workforce in an organization:

- Level 1: CEO, C-Class teams (HR, CIO, S&M, Finance)
- Level 2: Sr. Management, Directors
- Level 3: Line / Staff Managers and supervisors
- Level 4: Anyone else who is not in the first 3 levels.

Level 1 – Leadership

At this level, the following attributes would be formulated:

1. Vision: This would be the focus and reason to exist, its products and services. In a nutshell, it states this is about customers (consumers). i.e., an automaker like GM, the

main vision is to build and sell vehicles. (It could have other products and services, but this is the trade that it is known for.)

2. Goals: These attributes would outline, in a high-level manner, the purpose, its existence, its industry, its market, its geographical operation, and its short- and long-term strategies.
3. Objectives: these attributes would outline an actionable plan for the associated set of goals for each pillar or unit. Some of the key objectives are market and product analyses, risk portfolio, revenue and profit assessments, customer and partner management strategy, and a performance scorecard for leadership across core pillars. Each vision attribute would have targeted objectives for the creation and operation of its products and services, aligned with its intended vision.
4. Strategic attributes are a set of directives for each pillar: HRM, Finance, S&M, IT, and Management.

Level 2 – Sr. Management, Directors

This level would adopt the level 1 vision, goals, objectives, and strategies to structure its individual pillars. For example, Information Technology and Systems (IS/IT) would use the directives from level 1 to create the departmental vision, objectives, and strategies that would generate portfolios, programs, and projects for its pillar.

This level will translate the leadership vision and goals into actionable, measurable work to be performed as part of day-to-day activities. This level will be responsible for achieving the pillar's objectives. It is this level's responsibility to provide policy guidelines for the next level to follow, a directive.

This level also provides detailed processes for following the policy. For better efficiency and effectiveness, this action would be passed on to the next level.

Level 3 – Line / Staff Managers

It is the responsibility of this level team to provide a plan of action with detailed processes and procedures, based on the directives and policies provided by the Level 2.

This is the level that runs the operation, unbelievably. This level has a consequential effect on employees. This is where you would see the real showcase of the BAD (Blame, Attack, Deny) strategy.

In a major event or change, this level has the workforce's livelihood in its hands, determining who stays and who is let go. This level would report all related events or change actions, and the results, upward for evaluation and analysis of the individual pillar's performance. All the collected data and metrics, along with the results of the operation for each pillar, will be gathered and reported.

Have you ever noticed that your leadership has a piece of your report to your direct manager at the town hall meeting? Were you surprised to see your manager's name on the credit for your work? Do not be surprised; that is given and standard. What is not normal is that your manager would not give you any credit in your annual performance reviews. This type of situation has its own space to talk about and analyse, which this book will provide insight into.

The critical factor at this level is its reports and metrics, which indicate organizational performance.

This is the level considered the gateway through which the workforce enters or exits. This means that most workforce hiring and release would occur at this level. Some of the major impacts and risks happen at this level due to the BAD (Blame, Attack, Deny) strategy by the management team. You will read a very specific case exclusively on this BAD strategy in which a line manager hired only professionals, then fired them to mask a program-level failure that resulted in a mass layoff, or, another name for it: restructuring.

Level 4 – Anyone else who is not in the above levels.

The largest headcount in an organization comprises facility, technical, and departmental team members; engineers and support groups; accountants; and analysts. If you do not have any employees for whom you sign or approve their paychecks, you are at this level.

Note: Many job titles with the keyword “manager” do not have direct reports; they are simply team leads. They are at this level, but they are enjoying a manager’s favour.

This level uses the approved and provided policy and processes to complete the assigned tasks. (Warning: if this level creates its own policy and processes without approval of the higher levels, then there is a risk of failing under the given policy and processes, which would become a reason to be fired.)

The following illustration is a high-level functional view of an organization. It is one of many perspectives.

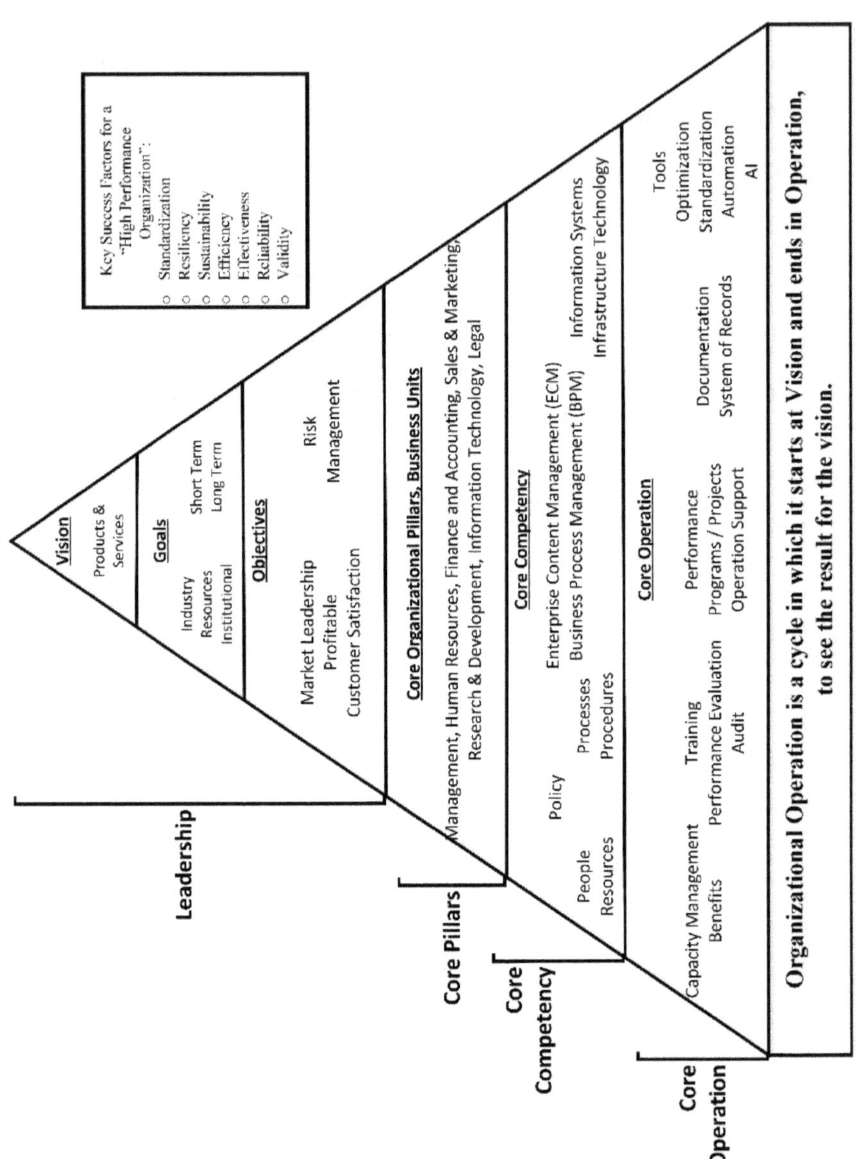

Figure 7 - Organizational Functions

Figure 7 Description: An organization could only claim that it is a "High Performance" rated if it could provide its key success factors through known industry standards frameworks.

Learning Maturity: This indicator assesses whether it is learning from its operational routines and approaching a level of maturity in which fewer problems occur and fewer recur.

Key Success Factors:

- Standardization: a coherent Policy, Process, and Procedures across all pillars, also called conformity.
- Resiliency: a level of adaptability to be able to resolve any major impacts, i.e., socio-economic change (recession), and quickly regain the norm.
- Sustainability: a business continuity rating that could endure any unwanted or negative changes to the workplace.
- Efficiency: a level of productivity that not only achieves the expected results but also does so at the lowest cost.
- Effectiveness: a rating for producing an expected result with the highest efficiency.
- Reliability: a quality factor for being accurate and consistent.
- Validity: a quality factor for information being factual and relevant.

oThis schema illustrates a strategy called "Management by Science." It routinely examines the current environment, captures metrics, evaluates actions and results from changes and events, and concludes with a series of improvement actions to be taken. Some of the most widely used standard frameworks with a high-performance rating are CMMI, Six Sigma, ITIL, TQM, and the Baldrige Performance Excellence. A combination of these frameworks will allow an organization to standardize its operations across content management, program and project management, auditing, and metrics evaluation. This action will create a workplace where all employees see their place at higher levels in Maslow's hierarchy of Needs.

An interpretation of Figure 7.

Leadership or executive class vs management class

CEO, CIO, CTO, CFO, and the list of C-class goes on and on. You will think there is logic and a scientific naming convention here. Well, there is none. It is merely an arbitrary naming convention of the organization, which entirely depends on it. It is done to avoid an issue, to start a new work stream, or to do something else. A case study will be provided when a director of an IT department decides to create a new title that excludes union membership. By doing so, she was able to remove union members in the same department by simply tagging their job titles as no longer needed. It worked, and it ruined union members' careers.

You might hear this name: Divisional CIO, Divisional CFO, or US-CFO, rather than just a simple acronym. It is not that the function has been divided, no. It is merely an HRM Strategic naming for that Global organization to give a sense of independence, while the host country would always retain final authority.

This management class lays out the roadmap for managing directors and management teams to follow. Each C-Class member will have its own pillar with all associated features and characteristics.

Disclaimer: This book has no targeted organizational classification, whether public or private. The intention is not to teach business entities and their features, but to provide a general review of a business.

To better understand the structure in relation to its workforce and workplace, the following basic task definition is needed.

This is the key element to understanding job performance discussion. This is where you, as a working-class member, must know so that you can survive any job performance tools, evaluations, or results.

In general, when speaking of a single task, there are basic levels of functions that would be engaged, affected, or considered in taking that task from its starting point to its completion.

The task initiation could be any of the following sources:

- A customer request for a service or product
- A maintenance request
- A new product or service line of business to be created
- A regulatory trigger causing a change
- An industry trigger causing a change
- A resource trigger causing a change

You might have other variables in mind. Please look carefully at the nature of the variable and see if there is any connection between your variable and the above initiatives.

Once a task is initiated, it will have a lifecycle within the organization. Each pillar will have a stake in the task's cycle, including impact, risk, ownership, and need-to-know. There are two types of structures to illustrate here: strategic and tactical.

Strategic Organizational Operation would address the following questions about a task:

- What is the task?
- Why do we need to perform the task?

- What is the benefit of doing the task?
- What is the cost of doing the task?
- What is the trigger of the task? Initiation –
- Which pillar is responsible for it?

This is where the task would be assessed against its needs.

To connect the dots, the following diagram is an illustration of workstreams side by side for Strategic Organizational Operation:

Strategic Organizational Operation				
Pillars	Level 1	Level 2	Level 3	Level 4
CEO / Owner	Vision			
Human Resources Finance Legal Sales & Marketing IS/IT Research & Development	Goals, Objectives & Strategy	Portfolio, Programs, Projects, & Policy	Processes & Procedures	Operation, Metrics, Audit, Report, Improvements

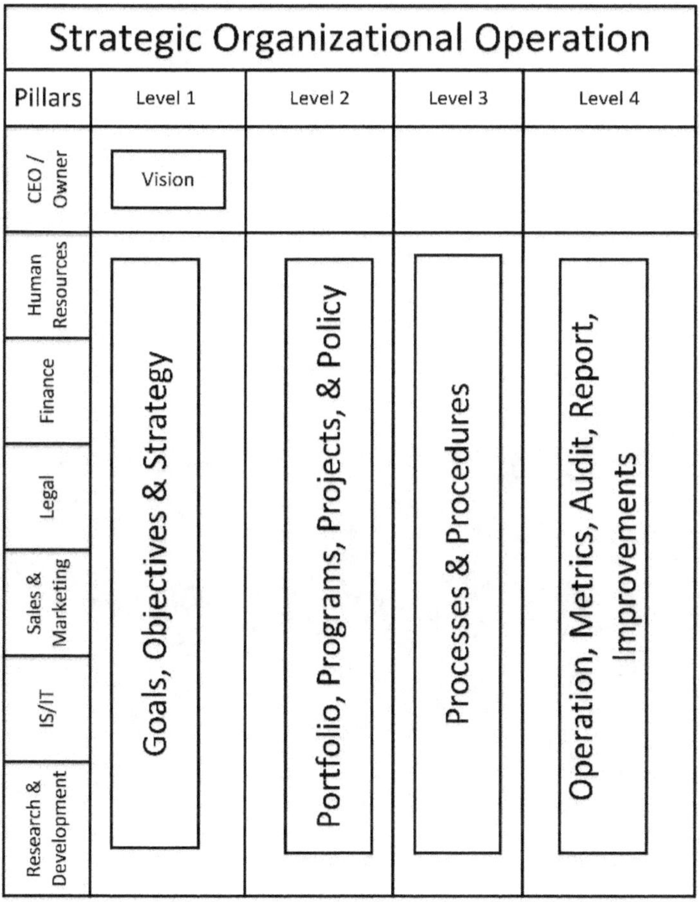

Figure 8 - Strategic Organizational Operation

Figure 8 Description: This structure is a basic and holistic view of an organization. There is variation in names and pillar designations, which would not match the above structure. At the same time, the functions in the above structure, regardless of their designation, would always remain.

Within each pillar, a set of attributes is in motion as part of its business function.

Tactical Organizational Operation would address the following questions about a task:

- What are the underlying policies, processes, and procedures to perform the task?
- Where does this task belong in the operational lifecycle?
- What are the expected goals and objectives around this task?
- Where are the policies, processes, and procedures to perform this task?
- Who is responsible, which pillar, department, team, to complete this task?
- What is the priority of the task?
- When should the task be started and when should it be finished?
- What are the metrics, expected reports, and results?

This is where the task will be performed.

The following illustration outlines a general Tactical Organizational Operation with its pillars:

Figure 9 - Tactical Organizational Operation

Figure 9 Description: Each level will be responsible for the functions that relate to the tactical operation. At the first level, a set of directives will be passed to the next level for execution. In a perfect organizational setting, considering its Operational Excellence and High Performance, there will be a clear path from Level 1 all the way to Level 4, and back.

The strategy and objective are interchangeable, depending on leadership perspective:

- What is the strategy to accomplish objectives?

- The answer to this question would be at the tactical level.
- What is the strategy for the vision at hand?

The answer to this question would be looked at in three dimensions:

1. Industry: What products and services are needed?
2. Resources: What material and capital are needed?
3. Institutional: What laws and regulations must be considered?

You were just introduced to two organizational concepts:

- Strategic Operation
- Tactical Operation

Both above concepts have the same high-level characteristics:

1. Formulate a plan of action
2. Implement the plan of action
3. Evaluate the result of the action

In any structure, there must be checks and balances to evaluate the initial vision and its objectives throughout implementation, and to gather results for an assessment of year-end achievements.

In the following figure, the Operational Landscape is another view of an organization's operations across functional categories at each pillar and level, providing one final holistic view of the structure before entering individual pillars.

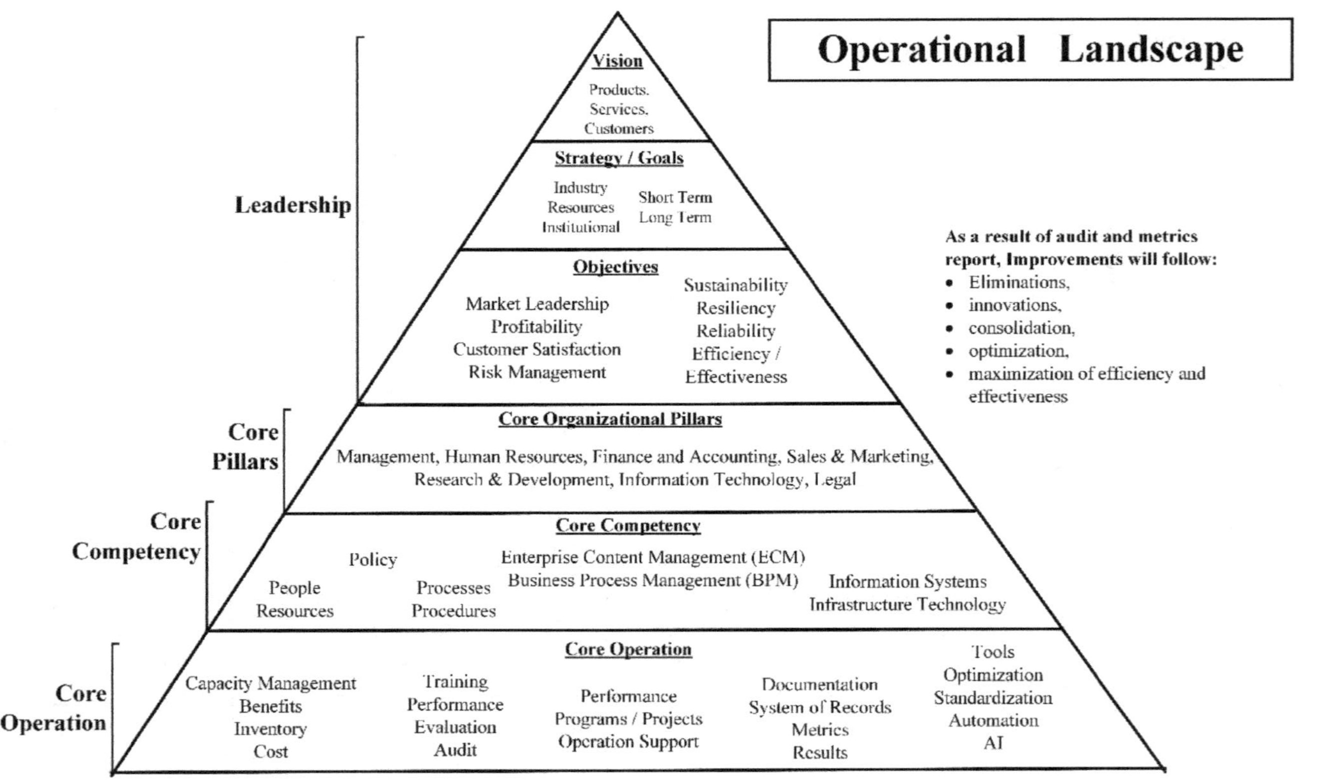

Figure 10 - Operational Landscape

Figure 10 Description: Each section in the above pyramid has a set of functions that must be transparent to the next section. The only way to validate such transparency is through a Quality and Audit assessment that is valid and reliable. On the right-hand side of the diagram, you see the effect of such transparency: an outline of improvements to help the organization make a course correction on time and prevent a catastrophic event, such as financial impacts from cost-cutting that will be passed down to the working class.

Please note that the above illustration is a snapshot of the entire workplace, yet it serves as a roadmap to help one understand the big picture.

In Summary

An organization could be any of the following entities:

- A small local company or business
- A global multi-unit corporation
- A government agency, local, State, or Federal
- A health care entity
- An educational entity
- etc.

Regardless of its type, it has a structure that ranges from simple to complex.

In general, the basic functions remain the same regardless of the size. You might see only one department, with all functions within it. On the other end of the spectrum, you could see a global footprint, including divisional and geographical units.

Now, let us read about each pillar and its high-level characteristics.

Chapter 2: Leadership

In this chapter, you will have an overview of leadership space, WHAT HAPPENS BEHIND THE CLOSED DOORS. This chapter and the remaining chapters in this volume will provide a consolidated overview of the academic and experiential aspects of leadership and management.

This group comprises so-called C-Level members. They include the board members, the CEO or President, and an array of C-level members who, in most cases, oversee the organization's decision-making, such as the Chief Information Officer (CIO) of the Information Technology pillar. This group either initiates or considers others' input on the vision and goals. They set strategic values and send them to the next unit to deliver.

The leadership style would dominate the rest. In general, there are three styles of leadership: Autocratic, democratic, and free rein.

Interestingly, many companies in the United States are practicing all three types. The author has personally worked under each of these leadership styles, both in the United States and abroad. Some of the cases in this book are, in fact, influenced by all of these styles, which, in some cases, resulted in bankruptcy or the failure of a major enterprise program.

Understanding the style of leadership would give you, as a working-class member, insight into what some of the triggers for leadership decisions look like and their impacts on your job and career.

This group includes those who develop strategic plans, evaluate competitive differentiation, address ethical dilemmas, assess the organization's economic performance, and look at the global picture to foresee future business and progress, keeping the company moving forward. Of course, this does not always work as outlined.

This space includes three major landscapes:

1. Organization: What happens at the highest level? the drivers and triggers
2. Leadership: How does the formulation of all directives come together? The vision, goals, objectives, and strategy
3. Management: the 5 Ws of how the vision is being accomplished

Organization

At the highest level, which you could think of as an existential purpose, the organization must define the following criteria:

- **Competitive differentiation**: for it to exist, it must have a product or a service for which there exists a customer who is willing to compensate or pay for the product or the service:
  - Customer domain: the marketing and sales departments would draw their visions and goals from the leadership team to formulate their strategy to conduct a complex consumer analysis in alignment with the products and services. This department set the stage for all other departments as to what was needed to continue its business.

    Without a customer to buy your product or service, your company will not last long. Even for new businesses that count on the first three years without profit and accept losses, there must still be some consumers for whom the company can estimate growth. It took some organizations years to achieve profitability. (Research the internet or libraries for companies that must wait for years, even beyond the academic standards of a 3-year program.)

  - Efficiency and effectiveness in operation: these two quality elements, as to how its products and services are being created, would have a significant impact on its marketing and sales department's success. Through efficiency, an operation would gain a competitive edge if its products or services cost less than those of its rivals' comparable offerings. Efficiency must not compromise the quality of a product or service. The most visible and common event is an automaker's recall of millions of its cars. By rushing a product and bypassing some of Quality Assurance (QA) steps, an audit factor in the line of production, to deliver faster to the market, an automaker would have sacrificed a quality for an efficiency of faster delivery, resulting a recall which would translate into a higher operational cost, and loss of revenue, as well as reputational factor which would impact future sales. The same philosophy works for other industries, such as software companies.

- **Innovation**: This is yet another key element for an organization to continue its existence. When the first two competitive differentiation attributes are accomplished for a new product or service, with quality and efficiency in production, having customers ready to buy the new product would be the success. As society changes, so does the demand for new products and services. Therefore, an innovative organization would be a frontrunner in a fast-changing society with evolving demands. You could only guess what would happen to a company whose products and services become outdated and no longer meet the present demands.

> Sometimes an innovation is what a customer thinks it is, whether or not the product is an innovation.

- **Economic performance**: This is the resiliency of an organization. They have tried various ways to achieve "Operational Excellence" across product and service creation and support, with a focus on defining their customers, improving efficiency, and enhancing quality. Yet when a socio-economic event, such as a recession, occurs, the reality of its "Operational Excellence" would be put to the test.

  How an organization responds to a change, such as an institutional, industry, or resource-based change, would demonstrate its resilience for survival. A mass layoff is the number one reason for the lack of resiliency. Let us give an example.

You are in a spaceship in space, and suddenly your operational chief tells you that there is not enough fuel to get back to Earth, unless the ship loses some weight. What would you say or do as a leader? Would you open the hatch and throw some crew out into space after you ran out of the cargo weight that wasn't needed? Or do you work with your crew to explore the options for getting everyone back to Earth? Even if that means losing your cargo and all other materials at the organization's cost? What if you go bankrupt if you do that? Which path would you take?

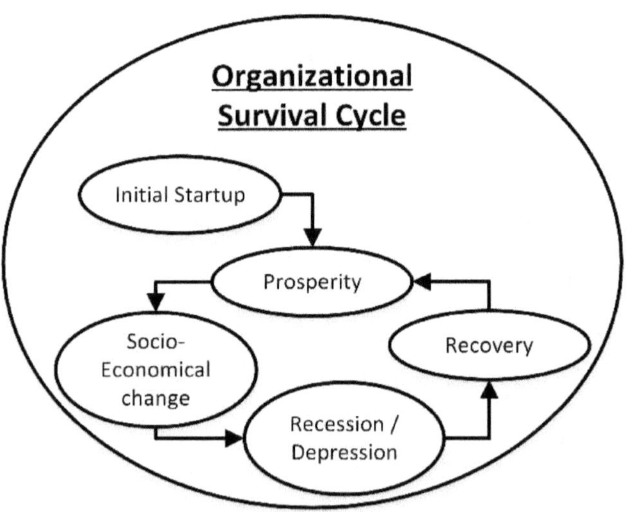

Figure 11 - Organizational Survival Cycle

Figure 11 Description: For an organization to survive, there are stages in its lifecycle that must be managed strategically. From its initial startup, there must be a strategy at each stage of its lifecycle to ensure it remains sustainable and operational. After startup, the company will enter a prosperity stage. When there is a socio-economic change, such as a recession, the organization must be resilient to survive the hard times and get back on its feet during the recovery stage.

The leadership team has an obligation for the organizational survival. Figure 11 depicts a cycle that is essential to an organization's survival.

There are strategies to prevent mass layoffs, but they are not profitable for a few or in the short term. If you research major society changes, like the 2000 Tech-Bubble, or the 2008 Housing and Financial collapse, you will find very few organizations that survived without even laying off a single employee.
An organization must have a strategy to follow this roadmap.

Without an economic performance strategy, a business cannot achieve the resilience needed for “Operational Excellence.” An example of that was a mass layoff by automotive companies in 2025 as part of the United

States' tariff strategy, resulting in a global shift for every automaker, from plant closures to forced early retirements and mass layoffs. There will be multiple cases around this change, and the strategies some organizations used to mask their mass layoffs. You will read about them in volume two.

Within an organizational hierarchy, there exists an element of risk that contains an attribute called contingency. An "Operational Excellence" philosophy without a detailed contingency plan is meaningless. This must be accounted for in any economic change, domestic or international.

Leaders and Managers

The members of this group are those who would set strategic goals and make them happen. They are the director-level members who make decisions over how exactly those objectives and goals should be accomplished. This group then hands off the directives to the next level of the operation to achieve tactical-level milestones and accomplish strategic goals.

This unit brings critical thinking and creativity to the table, as well as adaptability to change and resilience. This group would lay out the feasibility map for the leadership, whether the leaders' strategy would work, and what should be changed to make it happen.

Sometimes, a new strategy is born in this group and is adopted by leadership. This is the core body of an organization. This is where its true vision and goals are formulated and organized for implementation.

Summarizing leadership and management space into four major attributes, which would be demanded and expected of a leader or a manager:

- Competency
- Capability
- Characteristics
- Decision making

Competency

A leader would set the stage for the organization with a vision that drives it toward its goals and objectives. To do that, a leader must possess critical thinking and be creative. These are non-negotiable trades. As you will read further in this book, some cases illustrate a failure of vision due to a lack of critical thinking, resulting in yet another negative change, and impacting the working class.

This is the leader's critical thinking, which evaluates the adaptability needed to make the vision a realistic goal.

Capability

A Leader's capabilities are the key factor in establishing trust and credibility with the employees and top leadership. Too often, this abstract behavior from leaders has been put on display, including global leaders.

A lack of a leader's capability would result in catastrophic consequences for the organization. Here are some of the major capabilities for the top and middle management and supervisory roles:

- Skill set: technology savviness, human interaction, conceptual demonstration of a case at hand
- Functional characteristics: planning, organizing, directing, and controlling. (Common major phases of operation.)

There will be cases later in which you will read about the signs of a leader or manager who lacks the capabilities needed to perform their managerial duties.

Leaders Characteristics

Here are the common leadership or management styles:

- Autocratic
- Democratic
- Free rein

Each management style would work with the organization's cultures, principles, and values.

This is a combination of a leader's capabilities and competencies.

Some leaders consider the ethical dilemmas a side note when evaluating adaptability to a change. Here are some common dilemmas among leaders:

- Conflict of interest
- Honesty and integrity
- Whistleblowing
- Loyalty vs truth

(**Contemporary Business**, page 39, fig 2.3)

Note: For further details on this subject, use the books in the Reference section.

Decision Making

Finally, a manager's or leader's decision-making ability reflects the combination of all the layers mentioned above. This is true even when delegating decision-making, which is a decision in itself.

Note: The art of delegation is different from dumping the task on someone else.

Some of the common tasks of decision-making are:

1. Identify problems and opportunities
2. Identify options
3. Evaluate options
4. Select the best option and implement it
5. Evaluate the outcomes

The above structure is the foundation of the problem-solving strategy. It is also a core thought process for a visionary to see a need or demand in society and figure out how to satisfy it, treating it as a problem to be solved.

Aside from the four major attributes above, leaders and managers also have functional traits.

Away from the organizational body and its leadership team, the next layer of management teams is those who take the charter from the leadership and proceed with its implementation.

To keep it simple, the academic area has outlined the simplest structure that I have seen among academic textbooks, as well as the real corporate structure for this layer.

In general, the following table outlines the management functions; to be more concise, it lists the most relevant functions that management deals with.

Table 1 - Management Functions

Management Types	Characteristics
Strategy and Planning	• Define mission, per pillar • Assess market position • Set objectives • Create market strategy • Set goals • Evaluate results
Teams Building	• Consider size, diversity, and level • Exhibit Tasks level functions: problem solving, cross-functional, and virtual cooperation • Manage team lifecycle: form, norm, perform, adjust • Manage conflicts: antagonistic, cognitive, and effectiveness.
Crisis Management	• Stick to the facts • Acknowledge the problem, and explain a solution • Communicate clearly and transparently
Human Resource Management	• Motivate • Become a role model for performance • Management teams • Manage a job Lifecycle: job description, recruitment, training, benefits, and separation

This plan will be passed on to the next management layer for execution and to provide status and reports.

As part of planning, the management team identifies teams for related pillars and departments. This team-building space, created by management, is also a key success factor for organizational objectives. If it is not done through a careful assessment of resources and skills, the result will not be pleasant.

A manager would consider all factors in team building, rather than a skewed view of traits. The most important competencies of a manager are:

- Conflict management
- Crisis management

The two competencies above can only be achieved by a manager or leader if the individual acts and behaves objectively in the face of the conflict or crisis at hand, without becoming subjective.

A quick focus on Human Resource Managers.

Resource management skills are yet another key success factor for a skilled manager. The Human Resource Management (HRM) team has evolved over its history. The origins of HR date back to 1900, stemming from work disputes and conflicts. In the 1980s, HR was more of an administrative function focused on the workforce and employment management. Moving into the 1990s and beyond, HR has become a strategic partner at the leadership table, aligning with management objectives rather than administering the workforce. The lifecycle management traits will be discussed later in this book, as they are directly linked to job performance and, in turn, to mass layoff strategies.

Due to HR's strategic alignment, the management team has significant influence over HR policies, processes, and procedures. This single alignment affects the workforce, leading to mass layoffs or other strategies and tactical actions aimed at the working class.

For the past two decades, the definitions of “Job motivation” and “Job performance” have evolved to align with organizational goals rather than workforce development. Very few of them are still leading the market with strong policies and strategies to motivate their workforces to achieve high performance, which could have led to more successful operations.

More on the subject of “motivation and performance” will appear later in this book series, through the related cases and the final volume, the summary.

For now, a high-level, performance structure would look like this:

- Set goals
- Set measurements
- Set feedback structures

- Evaluate
- Take actions: reward, no change, get rid of!

In all studies and research, you will not be able to find a lot of materials to answer this question:

> ➢ Why should there be a **need** for a performance review if an organization has an "Operational Excellence" result in all metrics?

In fact, if an organization is set up scientifically and systematically, from the first day on the job to the last day of retirement, an employee should perform as expected and improve as directed. It all depends on the top's strategic plans.

Job enlargement and enrichment have many strings attached. This HR Management Strategy would be discussed as part of cases that, by design, cause a workforce to fail, so that a termination for failure to perform would follow under the chosen strategy. This might sound alarming or concerning some readers, yet this is where the "Unwritten Policy" would be in effect.

After all, the purpose of this book is to help the workforce be smart and adapt to changes and events that affect an employee's job and career, such as mass layoffs.

In Summary

Put it all together for this leadership and management chapter.

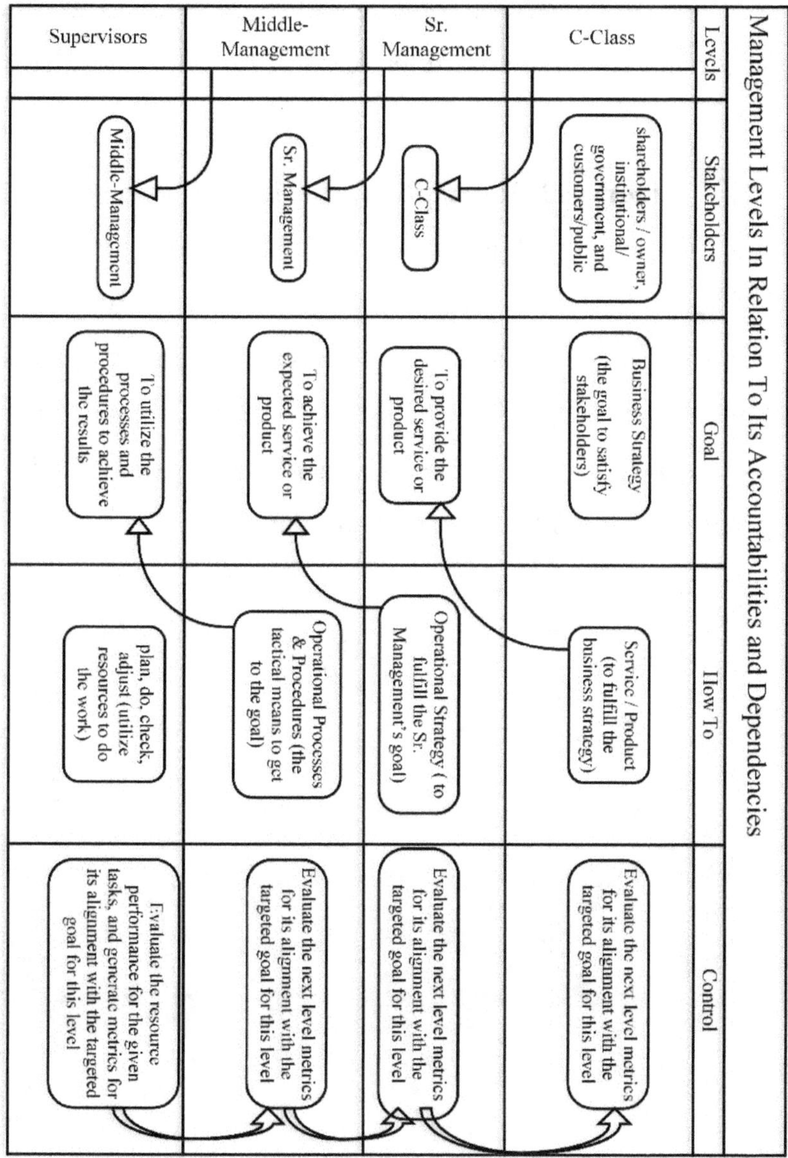

Figure 12 - Management Levels & Responsibilities

The previous illustration is a summary that could serve as a roadmap for some to follow. You could use the table below as a template to build on or simplify it further.

Figure 12 Description: A single illustration that could help you track a responsible pillar for a major change in your organization. A powerful tool helps the workforce identify pathways and interconnections among pillars, navigate causes and effects, risks and impacts, accountability and responsibility, and many other strategic and tactical functions that guide the overall structure.

Chapter 3:

Human Resource Management

The structure of this unit depends on the leadership arrangement. In general, the Human Resource unit is known for recruitment, training, benefits, and separation. This group has far more interaction with the entire organization than any other unit. This unit provides the processes and procedures for other units to engage in recruitment, performance evaluation, benefit package preparation, onboarding, and offboarding of a resource, among other functions.

One of the major functions of this unit is to monitor all employees' behavior and performance to ensure everyone is safe and that the workplace is not becoming a hostile environment.

The above paragraph is reliable regarding its actual policy, but not regarding its practices, which are called "unwritten policy". You will read a case about an HRM tactic, an unwritten policy, to eliminate a threat to a workplace by removing the victim and leaving the actual aggressor alone, based on the management team's favor. Reminder: this book is not just about presenting a rosy workplace; it provides the reality of a workplace through factual events.

Like any other pillar, the Human Resource unit/pillar, or department, has a core structure from within, away from its organizational integration:

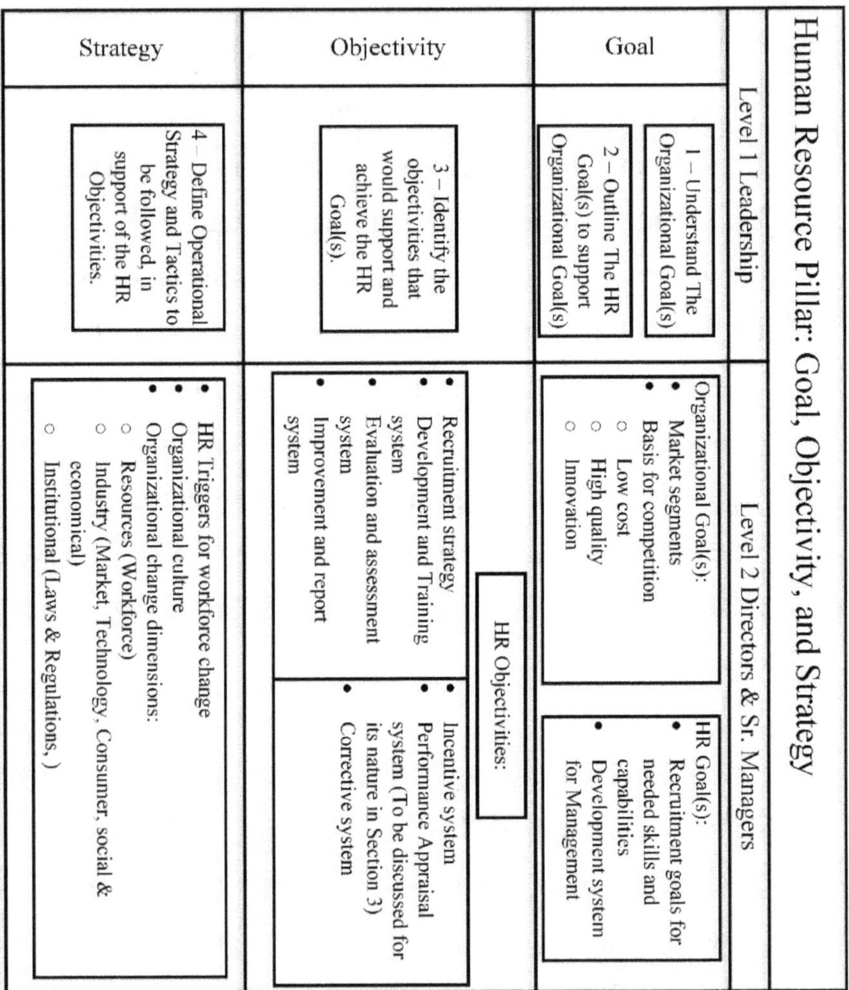

Figure 13 - HR Pillar: Goals, Objectives, and Strategy

Figure 13 Description: The above illustration is for a perfect HRM department. You can use this picture as a benchmark for your HRM to assess its performance. With that assessment, you would obtain the evolved HRM landscape since 2000. The major focus is on what leadership and management expect of it.

Note: the above framework would only work if the HRM had an independent role, thereby creating reliable and valid metrics and performance ratings, and generating an effective strategy.

One visible factor in HRM's low performance rating is a lack of consistency. An ever-changing policy based on unethical behavior by leadership or management would lead to a list of employee grievances. Bad morale among employees will affect their job performance. A problem with job performance will impact productivity. Low productivity means the efficiency and effectiveness of products and services are low. Low quality leads to customer dissatisfaction, which translates into lost revenue. In the end, it would be the business as a whole that would face the risk and impact.

There you have it, the domino effect of a bad manager.

Here is a simplified view of an HR space:

Strategic Planning			Execution	Evaluation	Improvement
Identify business goals and objectives	Define objectives and policies	Formulate action plans for workforce requirements	Implement plans	Analyze results against objectives	Implement corrective actions and improvements

The illustration above directly links to the organization's strategic objectives. Since there will be an impact on its workforce, HR involvement is inevitable; only the degree and level of engagement will differ. There are statistics on HRM that are used to discuss many of the textbook's contents. Unfortunately, the reality would not be printed, as it would conflict with what the HR reports.

In scientific discovery, data sets and information must be captured without external or internal influences to prevent unwanted biases that can introduce negative skewness.

The table below highlights the core functionality of a Human Resources pillar, from a tactical perspective. It is the simplest roadmap for HR to recruit the talent and expertise it needs to meet its skill-set requirements.

Table 2 - HR Basic Functions Roadmap

Criteria	High lights
Human Capital	Managing the knowledge, training, education, and expertise
SHRM (Strategic HR Management) SWOT analysis	Internal: Strengths and Weaknesses

	External: Threat and Opportunities To maintain a competitive advantage, HR must conduct a SWOT analysis to assess its workforce skills.
Productivity and performance measurements	Absentee rate, turnover rate, cost per hire, time to fill, HR expenses
Globalization Strategy	Lower cost, more productivity, higher performance, and an expansion plan

Strategic HR Management

The above table could be explained in multiple chapters and even books, which we will use to illustrate some common events.

HR's strategic structure has evolved to better align with leadership's visions and objectives. Today's HR pillar is no longer focusing on a workforce, or so-called employees. The HR believes, as multiple managers in multiple organizations indicated in a statement, "there are hundreds of resources like you lined up outside for the same job." This is a tough reality that today's workforce must accept and work with.

This is yet another reason this book has been written: to provide a strategy for the working class to navigate their workplace toward safer, more secure employment.

A greater focus on loyalty and availability has taken precedence over effectiveness and efficiency, the two key elements of a "High Performance" organization, resulting in an "Operational Excellence" status.

The definition of loyalty is "to do what you are asked to do, without questioning the legality or ethical circumstances of an action."

The "Availability" factor has long been used by management teams, dating back to the early 1900s, the age of manufacturing.

If you are not available, that means you are not useful to the company. Ask yourself, why does your company have so many events to keep you busy, even to the point of keeping you away from doing your assigned tasks?

Is that a good thing or a bad thing to always be available at the manager's demand? This point will be discussed during performance management cases.

Similarly, availability is defined as a resource being available 24/7, even on holidays and vacations. This strategy has trackable evidence of impact on the quality of work performed, causing highly skilled employees to leave for better opportunities, impacting system uptime due to long hours and recurring problems from a lack of routine maintenance, and reducing the organization's productivity.

In a place where availability is more important than the skills and capabilities of a resource, you would notice that more subjective practices are played by management teams, especially during performance ratings and bonus calculations. It is a question of whether a candidate favors a manager.

As a Sr. manager once mentioned in a departmental meeting while congratulating the newly promoted individual: “Do not worry, we will all help you!” This was mentioned after the individual herself said she neither had the skills needed for the new position nor any experience in that field. It was a clear case of the Sr. manager's subjectivity in promoting a favored individual and making everyone else know they needed to help her succeed. For a highly visible position at a Sr. management level, a new candidate should at least have some knowledge of the task at hand. That is called “capability and competency” at hand. The selection was purely based on the personal relationship with the individual.

Creating a scorecard for each pillar would bring value-added metrics to the HR department. Without internal transparency, any HR statistics shared with external entities would be considered biased.

One of the key values of this book is to provide an internal insight into its pillars, rather than a simple academic depiction, to show the reality of each pillar in action.

You will read about a case scenario in which a report to the HR team about management misconduct was not only ignored but also resulted in the employee who made the report being terminated. The reason is pure loyalty and favoritism, putting loyalty and unethical behavior ahead of best practices, efficiency, and effectiveness in job performance, and finally, ahead of customer satisfaction, thereby impacting production and services.

To make sure that the purpose of this chapter is clear. You are reading about HR strategy and tactics for the workforce, employees, staff, and line managers, as well as job performance ratings and evaluations. There will be an explanation of the relationship between mass layoffs or terminations and job performance ratings. The critical factor for you, as a member of the working class, is to strategize your day-to-day job so you are prepared for any termination and for subjective actions by management and HR teams.

Most basic HR functions, such as creating job descriptions, have been delegated to hiring managers. You might say: “Only the hiring manager would know what the 'need' is for hiring someone.”

You are right, yet in the old HRM, part of HR's work involved evaluating a manager's request for a new employee. HR would analyze the job description provided by the manager and assess whether a current one is in place, preventing any abuse of job elimination if the function remains the same. It was not about protecting union members, but about protecting an existing employee from a manager's retaliation or personal bias.

There is a strategy in the tactical aspect of a job description. i.e., to terminate an employee without breaking any laws. All the manager needs to do is label the current job title as no longer needed and create a new job title with the exact tasks and workload. This has been a practice for decades, in several organizations. It is almost untraceable to any audit, yet a detailed 3rd-party auditor could easily pinpoint it.

Without HR protection against such employment exploitation, managers have a free hand to do as they wish, without any consequences, ignoring laws and ethical dilemmas. Interestingly, in some cases, the organization was hurt; in multiple cases, different departmental programs were affected to the point of program closures due to financial losses and reduced productivity.

Quantifiable Hiring

The expectation for a new position, even an entry-level one, is that the employee is willing to spend their own time and money to obtain the needed skills and training.

- What is the key factor of hiring someone who does not have the skill set needed for a job?
- Have you seen a newly hired individual become a shadow of an SME for months?
- Have you seen a new hire with experience being expected to deliver results and accomplishments within weeks, if not days?
- What is the difference?

The answer depends on many variables. In some cases, bringing an intern is a normal and ideal way to add to the workforce. Aside from an internship, back in the day, bringing someone on board with less experience or education was also common, provided the individual was on track to obtain the expertise needed at the time. Lastly, but not least, are those with connections, friends, and family members who are loyal and available. If you are new in the office space, you need to get used to it. This is very common. Having said that, some focus on hiring far beyond loyalty and friendship, and more on skills and education. In some organizations, there exists a mix of both types of hiring.

This is where you, as a working-class member, should be aware, focus on your career rather than such office-related politics and behavior, and know how to navigate such characteristics in the workplace. In volumes 2 and 3 of this book edition, you will be introduced to strategies to manage such office-related events.

Despite the loyalty and availability schema, some recruitment strategies ignore both factors. One major example is for a change, such as mergers and acquisitions, separations, takeovers, or the creation of a new entity. These changes require a massive number of resources, in a very short time, to achieve short-term goals and objectives.

The interview and selection of policies and processes differ among organizations. How HRM poses interview questions, as well as in mid-year or annual performance review sessions, will define and shape their candidate selection strategy. Notice the author did not mention "candidate selection POLICY", as this HRM function is, in most cases, an unwritten policy, regardless of what you read or see.

The size of an organization matters in relation to these two factors. Being global has definitely clouded the personal effects on managers. As you will read in cases, a global entity with a local presence managed by a small group would have free rein to do what they desire, even to the point of masking a program failure due to a lack of competency of the management team in charge, and blaming that on the rank and file.

After the initial hiring comes the orientation. The orientation process has also evolved, from 90-day training to next-day performance expectations. HRM and management teams have learned that by shifting training and learning to new employees, they not only save money but also get an immediate return, as new employees work 24/7 to generate the expected productivity. Of course, this is not always the case, and there is no immediate productivity.

The old learning curve was used to forecast the cost of a new employee while they were still learning on the job. That curve almost does not exist in new hiring strategies.

There are still organizations with extensive training and guidance for the new employees, an investment that not many are willing to make these days.

One very specific: the training, the performance, and the objectives are all aligned within a 3% margin of error, in a high-performance organization.

The focus of this on HRM is on the following:

- Recruitment, initial hiring, and training policy
- Job performance management
- HR Strategic Pay Plan
- Separation, termination, retirement

These specific focuses are the major milestones for managing its human resources and talent.

Recruitment, initial hiring, and training policy

HRM can be examined from many angles. Here are some observations during decades of employment around hiring strategies for a single job posting:

- Hiring via Job Fairs
- Hiring via a direct replacement from the university's graduate list
- Hiring via word of mouth, from friends and family, a coworker, vendor, or a business partner, etc.
- Hiring via a contracting company, as a temporary or permanent worker
- Hiring internally, promotion, replacement, lateral move, demotion, to get rid of you, or as a favor, or because of loyalty

This action alone is the key to the rest of the organizational success, as well as employment practices. It defines how it connects its performance appraisals to a specific job.

Job performance management

In general, a core element of a job performance appraisal landscape would be:

- Identification of a business function
- Identification of the skill set needed to perform the function
- Formulation of a metric set for performing the function
- Assignment of an employee to perform the function
- Evaluation of the employee's performance is based on the set metrics.
- Appraisal of the employee

From the HR level, a so-called performance management landscape, these are the factors that HR deals with:

- HR performance management tool
- Organizational and departmental goals and objectives
- Individual employee's goals and objectives
- HR performance management ratings

For further reading on job performance, see the reference section for **Human Resources Management**, chapter 9.

Beyond a high-level overview of the HRM space, there is another view of it as more intertwined with the management team: a bottom-line view.

In this bottom-line view, three-dimensional categories define the HRM operational landscape, summarized in the table below.

Table 3 - HRM Dimensional Categories

Dimension	HRM Strategy Area
Value added	Benefit Package, Job alignment with the organizational goals, Control, and Audit.
Official	Laws and regulations, cultural norms, and HR practices
Ethical	Fairness of HR practices, validity, and reliability of HR Strategy

There are literally 100s of HR tools sold by vendors today, and they all include the above key elements in full. There are so many variations in performance ratings. To call out some:

- 20/70/10 strategy
- 360-degree feedback
- BARS (Behaviorally Anchored Rating Scales)
- 90 days to leave
- Paired Comparison
- Rank & yank

They are categorized both quantitatively and qualitatively. Yet either is being rated subjectively by the manager or supervisor in charge. One could easily argue about the validity and reliability of each key element in each organization.

Interestingly, when you question the validity of a system, the response will not be ideal from the HR team or the general manager. There is a special case of this behavioral aspect within both the HR and management teams at one of the author's recent workplaces.

HR Strategic Pay Plan

In old times, you worked 8 hours a day, then you got a paycheck on Fridays. That was your wages, benefits, etc., all in one piece of paper, a check to be cashed.

Now, there are so many variables and options that in some cases, if you blink and do not pay attention, your company's HR strategy will lock you in a default setting, with what would be the company's best interest, not yours. So, pay attention, research available options, and ask questions in writing before you accept a job.

Unfortunately, the old "trust" or the gentleman's agreement is no longer applicable to current norms. Companies engage in unethical practices wherever they can. If they see there is a way, they will do it. Reminder, even if that is illegal, it would be up to you to spend time and money to take any legal action. In an unethical case, if it is not illegal, that means an employer could do it. This is the harsh reality, not biased information.

There is a direct pay versus indirect pay, in the simplest way:

- Direct pay: paycheck, bonus, cash rewards, etc.
- Indirect pay: 401 (k), other investment options, healthcare, stock options, etc.

Compensation factors are:

- Experience level
- Educational degree
- Professional licenses and training
- Job performance
- Behavioral factors
- And lastly but not least, loyalty and favoritism

HR also employs motivational strategies, such as rewards, celebrations, extra bonuses, and extra holidays.

Separation, termination, retirement

This is a very wide area which could have its own book, literally.

The U.S. has an "At-Will" law, which allows both employers and employees to end employment at any time without cause. It is simple, in most cases, at the surface. But it is also complicated in some other cases. This notion of ending employment, especially by an employer, comes in various forms and names. To name some: mass layoffs, involuntary retirement, elimination of a job title, downsizing, and the list goes on and on.

Unfortunately, if one does not plan carefully, these types of terminations can have a severe impact on an employee's life, family, and career.

In Summary

The big picture in HRM space is the challenge to balance the three domains in an organization:

- Understanding the key factors that exist in an ever-changing market.
- HRM strategy to keep up with the leadership and management expectations for workforce allocation.
- A close watch over operations to understand the need for a robust workforce.

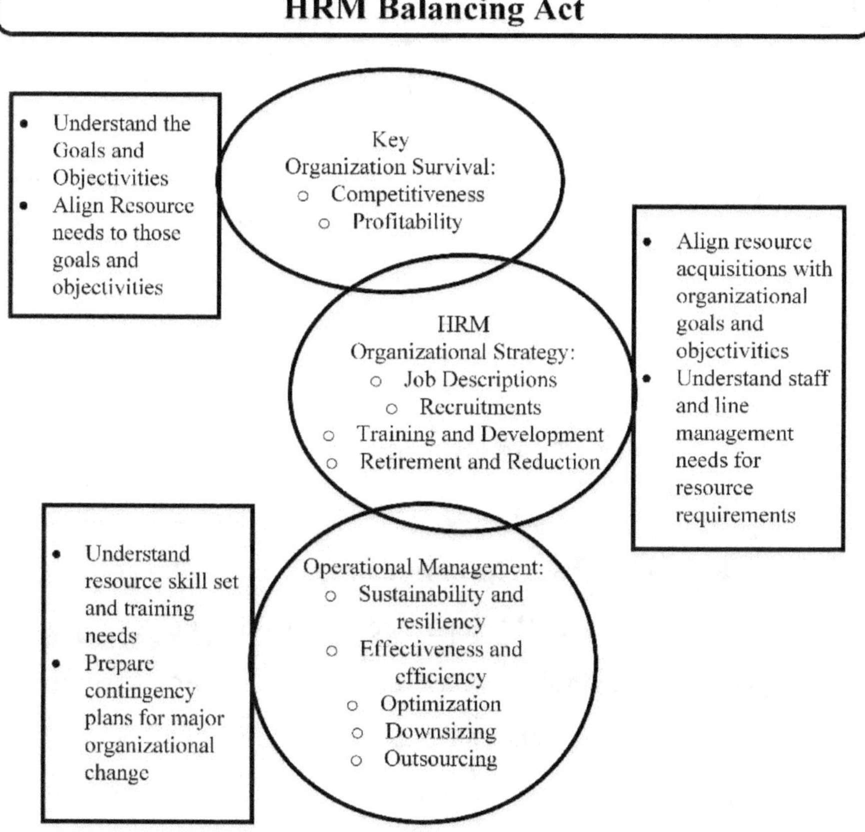

Figure 14 - HRM Balancing Act

An HRM score has been around for almost a century. The following table would provide the most effective and efficient ratings, with valid and reliable data to capture metrics with which an HRM could be rated.

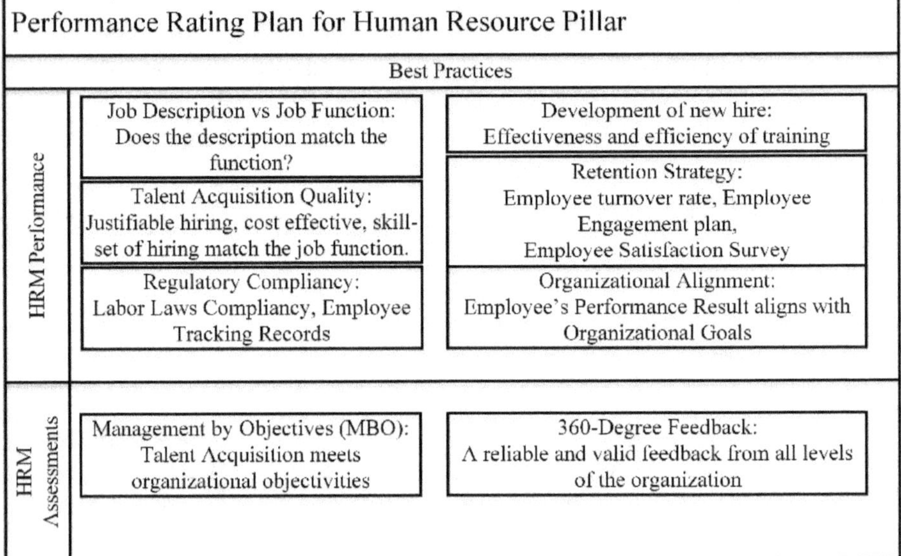

Figure 15 - Performance Rating for HRM

Figure 15 Description: This table consolidates the best practices in an HRM department. Unfortunately, only a few organizations follow such a schedule. Even in some global settings, this schedule will no longer work, per the existing evidence. One major reason is that personal favor and loyalty take precedent over skill set and expertise. The visible sign of such a workplace is the low performance and productivity. Although on one occasion, Sr. Management has been able to manually assign a rating to higher-up leadership that is not valid or reliable. Yet, they have been successful, to the point of financial trouble, resorting to yet another cost-saving excuse, eliminating some of the workforce to show a positive balance sheet.

There are two factors to evaluate a Human Resource Management team, or the department as a whole:

1. Assess HRM functions for their reliability and validity
2. Evaluate HRM results based on its effectiveness and efficiency

Unfortunately, without an independent audit and QA, it is impossible to provide valid metrics or to see the true results of their efficiency and effectiveness.

Chapter 4: Finance and Accounting

Without getting into too many details, this is the unit that keeps the organization going. In short, managing the money, what comes in vs. what goes out, and at the end, making sure there is enough left for the future changes to come, inflation, product or service setback, and of course, a possible recession.

Each unit of business will have its own budget to work with. At the leadership level, they will measure net profit to assess its future viability. This is where the units make decisions about resource changes or the best use of resources, keeping them at an optimized level and exchanging resources as needed, either by hiring or letting go.

Do you think your organization would ever initiate a mass layoff or any other HRM tactic to let go of a large number of employees, to save money to pay out to its executives and shareholders, ignoring any operational impact?

If your answer is: "They will never do that, because it will harm the company," then you need to read further, and look carefully.

Remember, an organization's survival is your job's safety and security as well, a two-sided blade. Therefore, the leadership, finance, and HRM teams must keep the overall budget on the positive side of the balance sheet.

This chapter will provide an overview of the structure of its finance and accounting pillars. Only basic information would be presented.

Every employee should know the basic financial strategy and accounting practices. After all, you will be paid if there is money left in accounting through a proper financial strategy; otherwise, the organization would be bankrupt, and you would be out the door with no paycheck.

(Yes, this has happened many times. You could search the internet for companies that went bankrupt and whose employees received no paychecks.)

Disclaimer: Not providing any company name here is to ensure there is no misrepresentation of the facts and no reputational damage.

Understanding the basic finance and accounting of your workplace would help you understand the triggers of major changes, such as bankruptcy and mass layoffs, Mergers & Acquisitions (M&A), takeovers, and Joint Ventures (JVs).

After the basic finance strategy and structure, the accounting structure and strategy come next, which would help employees understand how the finance works, in the form of paychecks, vendor, and partner payments.

One could interpret the difference between finance and accounting like this:

- The finance would focus on strategic goals, with an external view.
- The accounting would focus on tactical goals, with an internal view.

The above two elements must be in sync and balanced. A $1 billion strategic investment failure would have a major impact on the tactical layers. If the adjustment cannot be done on time, the consequences will be high for both the organization and the workforce. One direction would be bankruptcy, and the other would be mass layoffs, to either satisfy the debt collectors or cut operational costs quickly enough to reset revenue and net profit and save the operation.

Any failed investment would impact the workforce, no matter what. Every organization has a value, calculated based on its bonds, stocks, cash flow, net present values, and tangible vs intangible assets. It uses its values to generate revenue and cash flow by deciding which investments to make and which not to (opportunity cost). There exist policies and processes for decision-making, a so-called governance, as well as a reward for the decision, shareholders' profit.

You could find many books on this subject. The best recommendation is to handle each subject separately. To get started, here are two textbooks used in MBA studies:

- Principle of Corporate Finance and Accounting. You can find the book information in the reference section.

The takeaway from this chapter is to be aware of an enterprise's programs and investments. The size of a program really depends on its return value and cost. If the initial return value on an investment is calculated incorrectly, two things could happen:

1. Cost will exceed the calculated future value; therefore, disaster would follow if the program did not change its course on time.
2. The second route would be that the program's miscalculation would be lucky, and the calculated value would be less than the gained values; in that case, the organization would enjoy the prosperity. This also sheds light on taking calculated risks, which happen often.

Unfortunately, it is not that easy. To keep it simple, consider two factors:

- Static events, constant and steady things, will not change easily, and to some extent, they are reliable and sustainable to work with.
- Variable events, not static, not reliable, and for which there is low confidence in their sustainability.

Static elements include operational costs. A sudden change in the supply chain would for sure cause trouble in operational costs. On the other hand, variable elements are those not under the organization's control, such as tax hikes, supply chain cost changes, transportation costs (gas), resource costs, etc.

Financial management in a small bakery is not as complex as in a large corporation. The risk elements and the company risk tolerance for an investment endeavor vary from company to company. But, at the end of the day, the effect of a risk when that happens is the same on both types of organization, small or large. The importance of risk calculation and a mitigation plan is vital to survival.

Here is the principle of finance and accounting, in a nutshell:

Table 4 - Principles of Finance and Accounting

	Finance	Accounting
Goals	• Growth • Profitability • Maximize shareholder values	• Transparency • Compliance • Accounting illustration and accuracy
Strategic	• Plan for the future • Analyze financial data • Manage capital • Make strategic decisions (what will happen)	• Recording & reporting all financial transactions accurately (what happened)
Tactical	• Budgeting, forecast • Cash flow management • Capitol acquisition • Risk management • M&A, etc., support (Analyze data)	• General ledger entries • Bank reconciliation • Financial statements, balance sheet • Income statement, audit reports (Provide data)

Table 4 Description: The main functions of finance and accounting are to manage incoming and outgoing funds. There is no audit of internal allocations and justifications; simply accepting what each pillar hands over is the reality. Only a few had a finance team questioning spending by each pillar.

Note: This chapter provides an overview of the highlights of this pillar in relation to workplace changes and events.

The above table indicates the finance and accounting landscapes in general. If you would like to study this subject further, refer to the reference section for the related textbook information in your research.

An interesting perspective from the referenced book on these subjects is two things:

1. The seven most important ideas in finance
2. The ten unsolved problems in finance

The first one hints at the strategic landscape, and the second points to the tactical aspect of finance in action.

Overall, there are triggers that you could guess or estimate what would happen to an organization. Here is the tentative list of the triggers:

- Miscalculation of risks, failing a program. i.e., a lack of a risk strategy and a contingency plan for a large corporate enterprise program to replace IT platforms, which ended with a 180-degree course change, costing about $2 million.
- M&A failure due to the bad strategy and cultural conflict, i.e., lack of a leadership strategy, causing bankruptcy.

- Failed capital investment, i.e., automotive EV investment at the wrong time, due to the miscalculation of an institutional change.

Here is another perspective on a corporate finance strategy:

- Maximizing income and revenue (net value), in relation to the company's invested capital (products and services), by using the company's assets efficiently (materials and resources).

The lack of proper **planning** of programs and projects for product and service development is the most common reason for financial investment failure.

In Summary

The impact of a financial investment failure on the workforce is clear: cost-cutting factors. From there, you would be able to see what HRM position would be toward the cost-cutting, and how that impacts your employment as well as your career.

One major gap in organizational transparency is the finance team's lack of audits of other departments' operational expenses. They do the black and white of the work, finance, and accounting of what they are being handed over as an accounting book, rather than questioning the validity and reliability of the functions, as well as the efficiency and effectiveness of their actions, for the cost they incur.

With a list of expenses for account reconciliation in hand, the finance and accounting function is becoming a calculator.

In fact, there are cases where the finance team wants other departments to spend the money solely for next year's budget allocation. This has happened not only at the non-profit organization but also at the for-profit, a global one with its central office not in the U.S., a major flaw in finance and accounting, as the accounts are manipulated to show a budget that is beyond simple padding or contingency planning.

Chapter 5: Sales and Marketing

- Research and Development

Before presenting this chapter's subject, let us review a case scenario that will help to see the big picture for these two very dependent pillars.

Here is a story by the author to shed light on a business transformation that affected the workforce as a whole.

"My dad was a master tailor. Once, he said, "Do not assume everyone knows what exactly one wants to wear. Sell them something that they did not even know they wanted." That is the gist of a salesperson's intent.

Then, of course, there is the other side of the sale, a product or a service to offer. That is where the development of a product or service comes into play.

What do you think is the connection between an automaker and the dealership? Is it just like the automaker makes cars and the dealer sells them? Or do automakers work with dealers to learn what kinds of cars consumers are looking for? Considering the needs, wants, and wishes of consumers, you could imagine the list of demands.

In the clothing industry, it is hard for someone to find clothes that fit perfectly in any way and shape, except for those my dad made for his customers, because they were custom-made. But these days, due to the relatively low cost of materials, it is easy to find premade clothes that would fit your body type close to perfection, with an understanding of the cost variation.

Sales

Sales could be viewed as both an art (intangible) and a science (tangible). The art of selling could be:

- Being able to see the needs of customers and being able to produce a product or a service to match those needs, on time, at the right price. That would accomplish all the main variables of a successful business:
    - Right products and services for the right demand.
    - Affordable merchandise for the customers - cost efficiency
    - Timely delivery of the product or the service - competitiveness
    - Customer satisfaction, meeting the consumer's expectations of the products and services

Wait, there is another side of selling, the soft side:

- Long-term selling, retaining customers

- Honest business, customers are smarter than you think, and they will easily switch products.
- Building relationships, do not just sell the product for today's profit. Your customer today will have friends, family members, etc., which means a good salesperson would also be a good negotiator.

Marketing

For a small business, sales and marketing would be handled simultaneously by one person, probably the owner. In a larger business, strategic and tactical goals and objectives are distinct yet complementary.

Marketing could be translated into a simple outline:

- Have prepared goods and services
- Be able to deliver those goods and services on demand
- Be readily available, any location

It is the marketing department's job to avoid producing products or services that are not in demand, a concept known as "Marketing Myopia".

Marketing Strategy:

- Aligns with organizational vision, goals, and objectives

- Identifies a service or product to be made for sale
- Prepares a requisition for the Research and Development team

Research and Development teams initiate the creation of products and services. The sales team uses end-product information to create a sales portfolio for a campaign. A coherent illustration of the two pillars, S&M and R&D, could be presented in one chapter, as they depend heavily on one another.

An end-to-end cycle would look like this:

- The Marketing team will identify a product need: a mathematics book for the middle-school curriculum. After completing their work, the marketing department's output would be a portfolio, program, or project, which would then be handed over to the Research and Development teams.
- The R&D team will perform their work and prepare a product for sale. The output of this department would be the product and its description, which would be handed over to the Sales department.
- The Sales department will initiate a sales campaign to sell the product.

It sounds very simple. Well, in some cases it is, but in other cases it could be multi-year or multi-phase product development.

Who ensures the product meets the requirements provided by the marketing department?

You might ask yourself: What is the point of this chapter? You will see the connection later, but for now, know this: the failure of these two departments is, in fact, a major key in a disaster, impacting your job and career. You might not even know what happens if you miss the triggers.

A scenario: The Sales department receives the product and continues to build the sales campaign. Between the Sales and Marketing departments, one would receive customers' feedback on the new product.

Eventually, Marketing finds out that the product did not match the requirements. Now, you have a list of questions about what happened. Who was responsible for auditing the final product against the requirements? Why did the product reach the customer before it was audited for its requirements? Was there any audit at all? Or were there any checkpoints to make sure there was an audit? Or, did R&D mix up the requirements and create the wrong product? Who checks them out? Did they have an audit of their own products? Etc.

With this example, you will understand why these two pillars should be explained as one unit.

There is another factor in marketing and sales. Let us explore that with an example. Back in the early 90's, during the development of major computer platforms and software, many companies rushed to get their products out the door to the customers, to gain market share. In some cases, they failed on the first attempt, but their success was followed by market momentum, which culminated in an updated version of the same failed product.

Some would say those who took a risk and lost gained nothing. But the gain was far more than the single failure. An improvement in the development was made for some, yet a steady strategy was adopted. That strategy was: "Build as fast as you can, and send it out to customers. The fixes and updates will follow."

The speed of product or service delivery matters to the target consumer. A quick history review would reveal this fact. What was the first transportation invention? (Boat, train, bicycle, motorcycle, car, airplane, etc.) If you are due to receive $1 million, which method of transportation would you prefer? What if the delivery guy is next door? What if the delivery guy is on the other side of the ocean?

Delivering the right product at the right time to the right customer at the right location with an affordable price is the key to a successful business. The delivery of a base product matters, regardless of its success or failure. There is always tomorrow to fix it!

The takeaway here is that a company will have changes that would impact your employment, either in a good way or a bad way. If it fails to the point of bankruptcy, then you will be out of work. This is the company's operations that one should pay close attention to for their changes and events. Regardless of the change itself, your goal should always be clear:

- Do your best while still employed
- In parallel, prepare yourself for a sudden exit

Otherwise, you will be blindsided by the impact of a change, such as a major program failure, which would result in cost-cutting measures.

Product Development Structure

The outline is simple:

1. Initial product identification and requirements, done by the Marketing team
2. Product development and build-up, done by R&D
3. Finally, the product will be ready for consumers to buy, done by the Sales department

In a general view of the Sales and Marketing pillars, along with the Research and Development pillars, the illustration below would be a general landscape for these pillars:

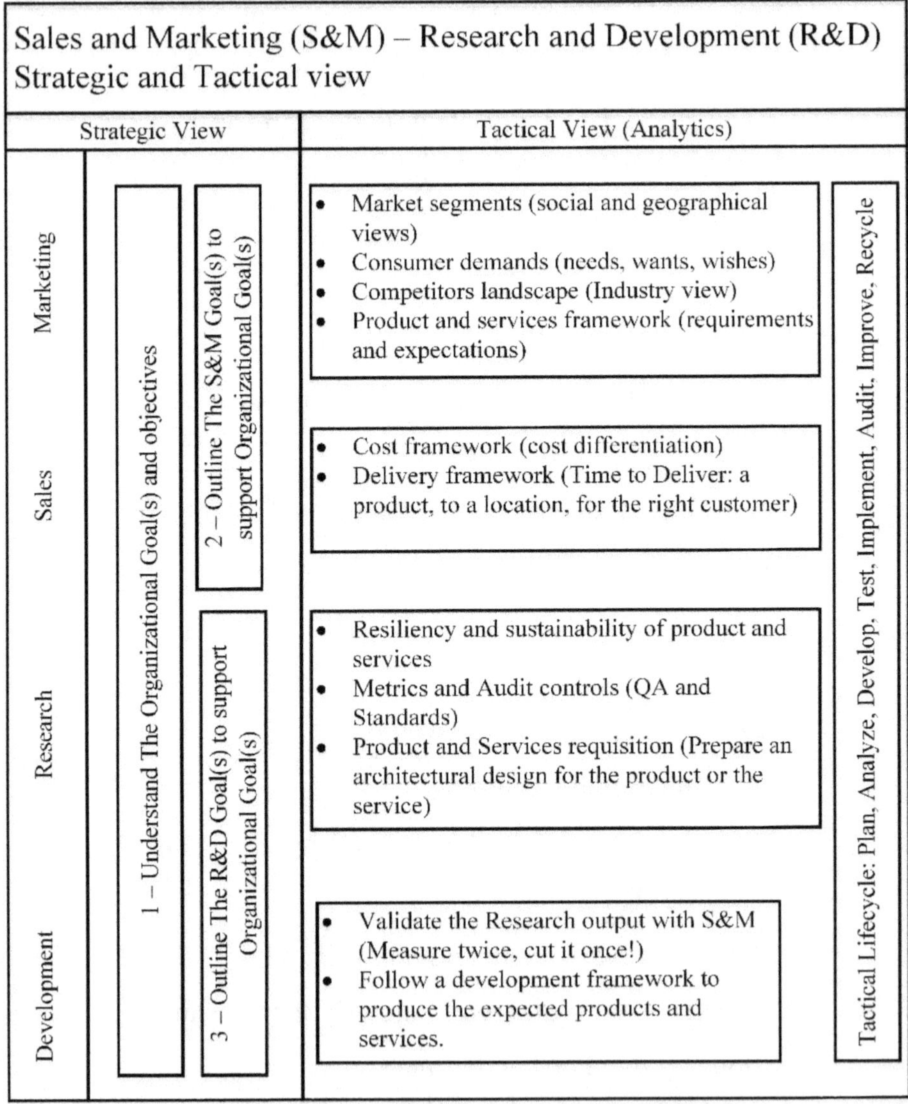

Figure 16 - Sales & Marketing Space

Figure 16 Description: what you are seeing in the above schedule is a consolidated multiple textbooks through the filtration of working experience. It is a footprint for best practices. At its core, it is designed to create the "Survival Cycle", Chapter 2, Figure 11, which you read previously.

Marketing plays a strategic role, and the rest are the tactical players.

The logistics of product and service development are:

- What is the process?
- Who is involved?

The overall product and service development could be summarized in a short outline:

- Phase 1: ideation (SWOT analysis)
    - Stage 1: generate ideas
    - Stage 2: screen for the best idea
- Phase 2: develop a new product, detailed design, test, and validation
- Phase 3: commercialize the new product

The following table provides a big-picture view. This table might seem very simple and basic, yet it is the foundation of an organization's existence.

Table 5 - Lifecycle of a new product or service

Stage / Phase	Ideation	Development	Commercialization
1	Brainstorm ideas, generate a list (SWOT)	Product definition	
2	Business case study and analysis	Prototyping	
3	Research and screen for the best idea	Detailed design	
4	Competition offerings and marketing	Develop and test the selected idea	
5	Supply, cost, pricing	Technology and Market development	
6	Prototype minimum cost	Validation and testing	Test the market
7	Total cost of products and services		Launch the product and services.
8			Evaluate, audit, optimize, and transform.

The success and failure of an organization's product or service depend on this schema of management and leadership.

The big picture for this chapter's pillars:

Table 5 will be explored and explained in volume 2, including its effectiveness and limitations when not followed properly. An existential decision-making toward a "right way" for a "right reason". Too many enterprise programs and projects failed to follow this schema to its core, resulting in negative organizational change.

Research and Development

This unit might not be clearly under R&D, but the related work does exist.

Without this unit, a business would fade away in time. Therefore, this unit must be well-organized and well-maintained so that future business keeps the business going.

There is a fine line in R&D spending: why would a company invest further in building a gas engine if an electric engine would replace it? That does not mean that no gas engine would be built anymore; it is just that its development would raise a big question, the answer to which is beyond the scope of this book. It goes back to the need for R&D and S&M pillars.

Stay close to this unit, as the nature of "IT Operational Excellence" will play a big role in it.

A change is a business change. To illustrate this from a strategic perspective, the following diagram presents an organizational change schema that could be used at any scale, in any local or global landscape.

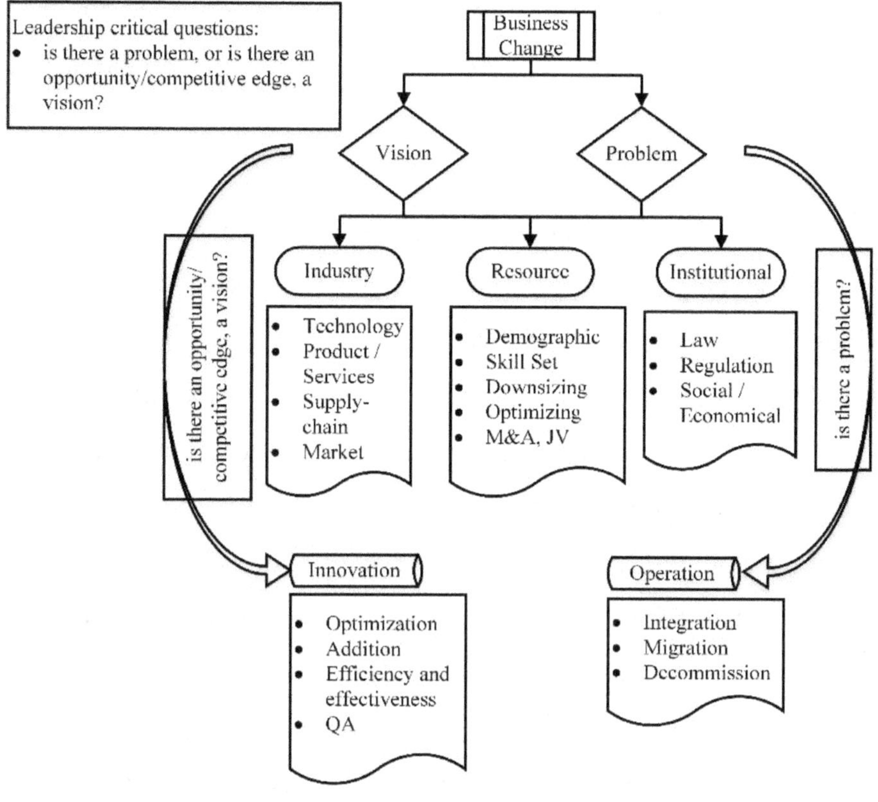

Figure 17 - Strategic Business Change

Figure 17 Description: A business change could be generated either via a new vision or a problem. Either could have a trigger from the industry, the resource, or the institutional spaces. The vision would become an innovation, while the problem would be an improvement or optimization within the operational space.

To connect this pillar to the workplace and employment in general, let us step into the development area for a moment.

Before the year 2000, most major organizations had their development teams in-house, providing so-called “in-house” products and services.

After the year 2000, with the rise of the internet and the birth of e-commerce, a major shift occurred. At the same time, the concept of outsourcing began to grow exponentially. Soon, In-house development was replaced with outsourcing, using a 3rd-party vendor as a source of needed services and products. Further down the road, after the year 2008, the recession, this outsourcing of products and services became an industry of its own, putting an organization's in-house development department further down on the history shelves.

With that industry change came a devastating impact on workplaces. The human resource, the working class, became furthermore a commodity rather than an individual; as a resource manager once said: “There are 100s of you waiting outside to get your job!”.

In short, you are replaceable in a heartbeat: there are 1000s of contracting and consulting companies outside who would take over your job the next day, including H-1 B visa resources.

Following the shift toward splitting the architect and engineering roles, they have been separated into two classifications:

- The Architect focuses on the business need
- The engineer focuses on the product and service

Before the year 2000, one person was easily in both roles. But, after the year 2000, the evolution of each title or role has continued into today's world.

An architect in technology would focus on delivering products and services as quickly as possible to meet market demand, which is what leadership today expects.

Unfortunately, what is not the same for the other role is an engineer. An engineer has been put on the spot to deliver on time, at the cost of quality, efficiency, and effectiveness, compromising reliability and sustainability.

Let us say it again, as this is a critical failure factor with their programs and projects:

- Delivering a service or a product to meet the market demand on time with the lowest cost possible, to the point of sacrificing quality, reliability, sustainability, efficiency, and effectiveness.

These are the key factors of "Operational Excellence" and a symbol of a "High Performance" team; they are all at risk.

As you will read in some of the cases in Volume 2, the QA (Quality Assurance) department no longer exists in most organizations as an independent entity. It is now a simple checklist for a manager to sign off on new products and services.

When was the last time you bought an electronic device, i.e., a laptop, cell phone, tablet, etc., that did not need an immediate update? (Note: a security update is also a factor in a failed QA.)

When was the last time you bought a car that did not get a recall within a year of operating it?

In Summary

By now, you can connect the dots between these pillars in this chapter, S&M and R&D, and the workforce employment workplace, and how important it is that you realize the triggers of those negative organizational changes, which would impact your employment and earnings, and job security.

A robust S&M would stay very close to the economy's overall changes, including those affecting its customers, to make reliable and valid decisions about creating a product or service. At the same time, an adaptable R&D would always seek improvements to existing products and services, to the point of retiring those that are not efficient or effective for the target customers.

Chapter 6: Information System / Information Technology (IS/IT)

All industries, banks, retail, healthcare, education, manufacturing, automotive, consulting, etc., have one major business pillar in common: Information Systems/Information Technology (IS/IT), one way or another.

We will explore the operational nature of this department to evaluate its strengths, weaknesses, and challenges, so that we can outline what “IT Operational Excellence” means and define a “High-Performance” organization.

The author’s experience began with programming a single DIP with 14 legs (pins) and has since spanned 40 years in the electronics industry, culminating in the management of a data center transformation. Reminder, electricity existed before the age of Information Systems and Information Technology.

You and the author might have different views on what the IS/IT definition is, yet it all comes down to 0s and 1s, which are generated by electrons, positive and negative. Creating the most sophisticated chip set today.

Just a general introduction for two most common terms in technology today.

What is an Information System?

- Any virtual entity that is not a physical layer of your laptop, cell phone, TV, etc., is called an Information System. That is mainly raw data and information across many different categories. The operating systems on your devices manage all the applications. The network layer of your devices that manages your network, WIFI, and your cell phone towers. Then comes the application layer, which is your main playground, your social media, such as Facebook, Twitter, etc. Security applications, such as McAfee, CrowdStrike, and Cloudflare, help protect your devices and the overall cyber landscape. Throughout the evolution of Information Systems, all these bits and pieces of virtual data and information have existed in files and databases, in encrypted or plain-text formats.

What is Information Technology?

- This is your physical device, the laptop, cellphone, tablet, etc. From the AT&T fiber cables coming to the Data Centers, the Data Centers farms of machines, IBM Mainframes, Dell servers, Oracle databases, and the list goes on, for all layers of the electronic landscape: networks, security, servers and databases, applications, etc. what was once pounds of metal and very expensive, called a PC (Personal Computer), has turned into a small, much more powerful and lighter physical device, a tablet on your hand to carry.

IS will not exist without its body, IT.
It would be like a soul without a body. An IT could exist without an IS, a brand-new chip set, not yet programmed. That is as small as it gets.

Today, there are not many communities around the world that lack cell phones, TVs, tablets, laptops, or any other electronics.

The 1st assumption of this book is that the reader, you, has some basic knowledge of technology, as well as those who are professionals in this industry. Also, it does not matter whether you work directly in an IS/IT department. You could be working in accounting or in HR. The principles apply to all workforce types and natures.

Before the year 2000, a Technology department called IS/IT, a mix of SW and HW, for its products and Services. IS was focusing on the soft side, software, and IT was focusing on the hard side, hardware.

The evolution of technology has enabled anyone with any level of skill or experience to do the job of an IS/IT specialist, such as an architect, an engineer, a developer, or a support technician. This is where the line between those who worked in IS/IT for decades and those who were the end users is, the customers of IS/IT members. This was and is the defining moment for anyone to learn how to do something that, at one time, only the IS/IT community could do.

In summary, here is the purpose of the technology:

- Allowing everyone to do what they need to do for the everyday tasks.

Now expand that last sentence into a global entity today.

The need for technology has expanded with an almost unlimited number of options and functions. The structure of an IS/IT pillar is pretty much the same across all industries.

To illustrate the overall view of an IS/IT pillar, which would be tailored per organizational needs and industry, the following diagram presents a broad view of this pillar:

Figure 18 - Overall IS/IT Pillar

CEO (President / Superintendent) and Board of Directors (Governance)

Organizational Pillars / Units
HRM
Finance and Accounting
Sales and Marketing
Legal

CIO (Chief Information Officer)
Organizational Architect
Research & Development
IS
Application Architect
Application Analyst
SW Engineers
SW Developers
SW Security Analyst
IS Test and QA
SW Implementers
SW Support
IT
Systems Architect
Systems Analyst
Systems Engineer
Database Architect
Database Engineer
Server Architect
Server Engineer
Security Architect
Security Engineer
Network Architect
Network Engineer
IT Test and QA
IT Deployment Teams
Data Center Facility Manager
Data Center Manager

Stakeholders: Business owners and consumers
PMO (GPMO) Program and Project Management Office
Procurement Team
Program Managers
Project Managers
Project Coordinators
PMO Control and Audit Teams
In-house and Outsourced Vendors

Figure 18 Description: Among dozens of organizations, the IS/IT department has a basic structure similar to this illustration. It is intertwined with all other branches and pillars. There is also a strong connection between the IS/IT department and other departments: any changes or events on either side would impact the other, without fail. For this reason, this content applies to any pillar.

The illustration above depicts the landscape of an IS/IT, including its integrations with other organizational pillars.

The enormous job description list across this single pillar will have its own book to write about. You will read about the major job description schema in the second volume, along with associated cases, and how management and HRM work together to control enterprise change.

By studying the illustration above, you can understand how this pillar is connected to all other organizational entities, pillars, and units.

Since 2000, the control and authority over this connection among the pillars have been fundamentally shifted. For one, it is no longer an IS/IT pillar that would direct the business on which tools it should use.

One simple example was the change that was an eye-opener back in the late 90's, when a business team member asked for a quick update to the customer-facing pricing list. Back then, the IS direction to business was to wait until the technology team planned and worked on it, while the business lost momentum on a market advantage to implement a business change. In early 2000, the same business member learned how to do that without the IS team, the first step forward for a business team to gain control of the IS, and better business management.

Regardless of your job title, the impact of an IS/IT change on your job is inevitable. Therefore, it is critical that you better understand the triggers of a business change and its impact on your job, so that you can prepare for the ultimate disaster: losing your job with one phone call while driving home from work at 5 pm on a Friday.

Just to shed some light, here is a sample of a team outside of an IS/IT pillar, a customer care call center. By implementing an automated system to take incoming calls, route customers to pre-made functions to obtain their account information, automate basic accounting functions, remove the need for even a single representative to take a call or help the customer, and balance their accounts. By implementing this very system, the accounting department manager could assess the headcount needed to support customers, eliminating excess headcounts.

Here is a general outline of a business change.

A CEO needs cash at hand for a vision to come true.

- Finance and Sales & Marketing teams work together to see the feasibility of raising cash and bringing the vision to reality.

- Sales and Marketing, including product and service owners, and Research and Development, along with IS/IT products and services owners, would work together to start the initial brainstorming of the vision requirements and needs.

  Note: there is business ownership, and then there is IS/IT ownership of a product or service. The business side would manage the customer/consumer side using applications and tools, while the IS/IT side would manage the SW/HW side that supports the application systems.
- Enterprise Architect (EA) would work with R&D and HRM to assess the needed resources and skills.
- Program Management Office (PMO) would work together to initiate a program to support the vision at hand.
- PMO would organize and work with IS/IT leadership to plan for an actionable work to be started.
- PMO would then deliver a set of projects to start working on the vision delivery.
- The project teams would then take the requirements from PMO and start working on the delivery of the expected results.

This is just a simple path from an idea or vision to the final result, a product or service. There are many different approaches, some simpler, and some very complex.

To demonstrate a “single task scope of work” that needs to be performed toward a vision achievement, the following illustration presents an integrated view of all stakeholders:

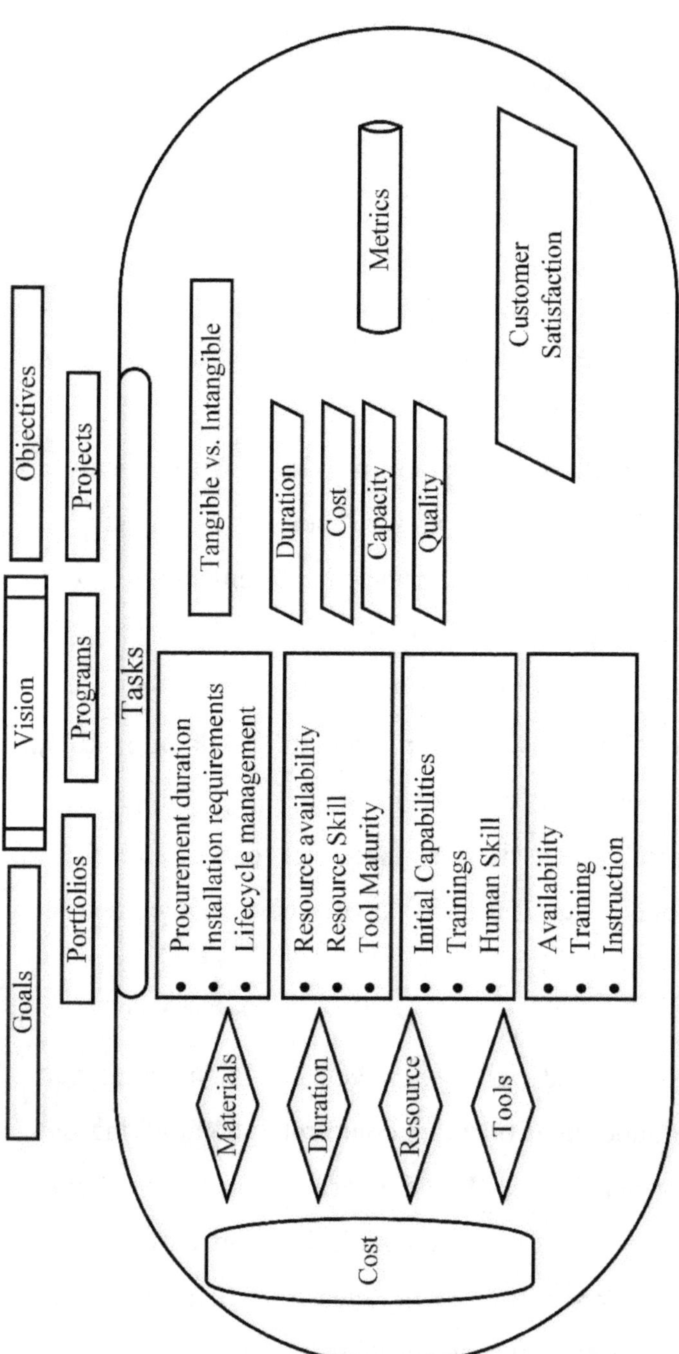

Figure 19 - Single Task Scope of Work

Figure 19 Description: Make sure you review the above illustration carefully, as it has a great deal of connection to your job performance review and protection. This is where you could build your story for your job performance.

Basically, it all comes down to a single task measurement, a unit of work, and how that unit of work is going to be assessed for your job performance. It all starts with the organizational goals and trickles down to a single task to be performed. All the above schema is telling is:

1. Know the objectives of your task in alignment with your departmental goal.
2. Know the expectation of the task for its results.
3. Accomplish the task with all available tools and skills, with efficiency and effectiveness.
4. Make sure to record your task event, end-to-end, from start to end. (That is the key to your performance review rating.)

If you get that right, you have a 100% guarantee that no HRM or supervisor of yours could rate you anything but a high performer. You will read a case in which the schema above not only saves an employee's low job performance ratings but also protects the employee from being punished by HRM, as neither the supervisor nor HRM could find anything to punish the employee.

When you go to a dealership to purchase a car or go into a bank to get a car loan, or even go into a bookstore to buy a book, you most likely would interact with a salesperson, with several different titles and tags. It seems simple enough, right?

Well, from a consumer perspective, yes, it is simple. But from the organization that created that product or service, it would take many people to deliver that new car or a new loan to the consumer. Beyond the first layer of creation, other layers operate in parallel to maintain and support the same product and service. Here are some depictions of the order in which events occur to drive an IS/IT change.

To illustrate what a change is, we need to understand the concept of Change Strategy. In the following figure, you can see the high-level of a Change Strategy. This is where you would ask for the reason for the change and justify it.

Now, let us look at this from a different perspective.

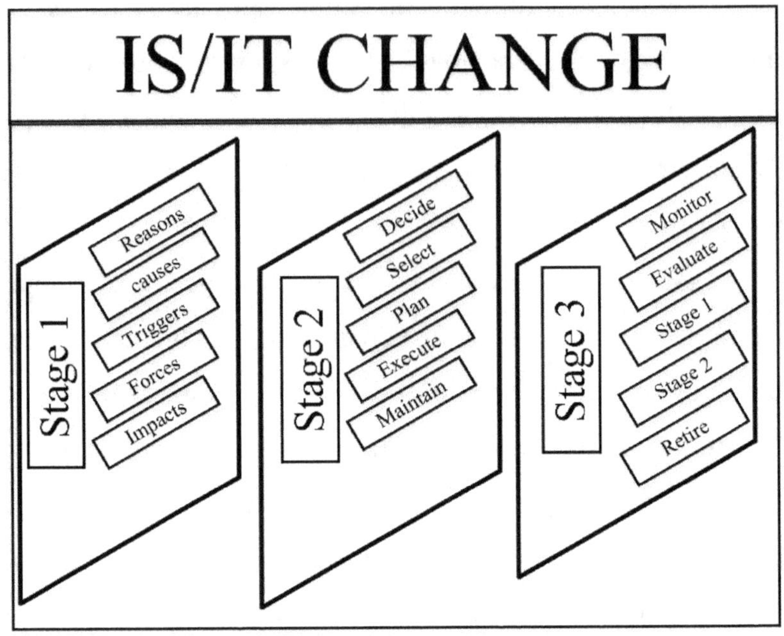

Figure 20 - IS/IT Change Stages

Figure 20 Description: To put the above illustration into perspective:

Stage 1: This is for the leadership team to set the stage for the change and to develop the reasoning and justification.

Stage 2: This is where all action starts, turning stage 1 into an actionable portfolio/program.

Stage 3: This is the sustain phase, the normal operational cycle.

One might call it a Change Lifecycle, rather than stages. It is the concept, not the naming, that matters.

In stage one, the critical element to consider is the reason for the change. After all, it is the reason that justifies the cost and effort of the change.

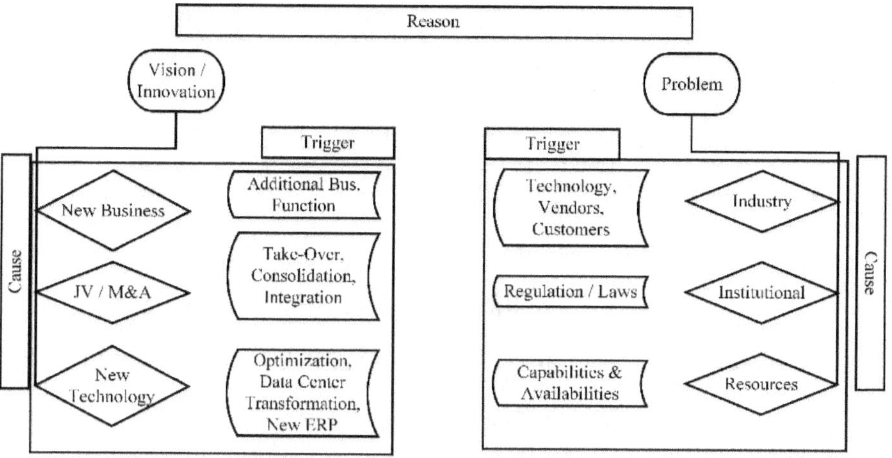

Figure 21 - Change Reasons

Figure 21 Description: This is the place for a workforce to look to identify a trigger for what is coming next, to impact their career and job. There are cases after cases, among all the organizations, where these above signs and triggers of the reason for the change would help you to navigate your career and job at any workplace.

As part of Stage 1, the leadership team meets with IS/IT owners to sync up and communicate the goals and expectations. (Vision/innovation)

The IS/IT department will initiate changes. Either way, the process is pretty much the same, the reasoning and justification for spending money.

Some key success factors for a change, from its origination to its completion:

- It is crucial that leadership and IT owners evaluate and audit their line of thinking and strategy post the initial communication.
- This step has proven that if it does not happen, a gap between leadership and IT owners will be created, which will harm the change down to the execution level.
- This step is a guarantee to make sure that all stakeholders are still in agreement and in alignment as to what the goals are to accomplish as part of the incoming change, and the expected results.

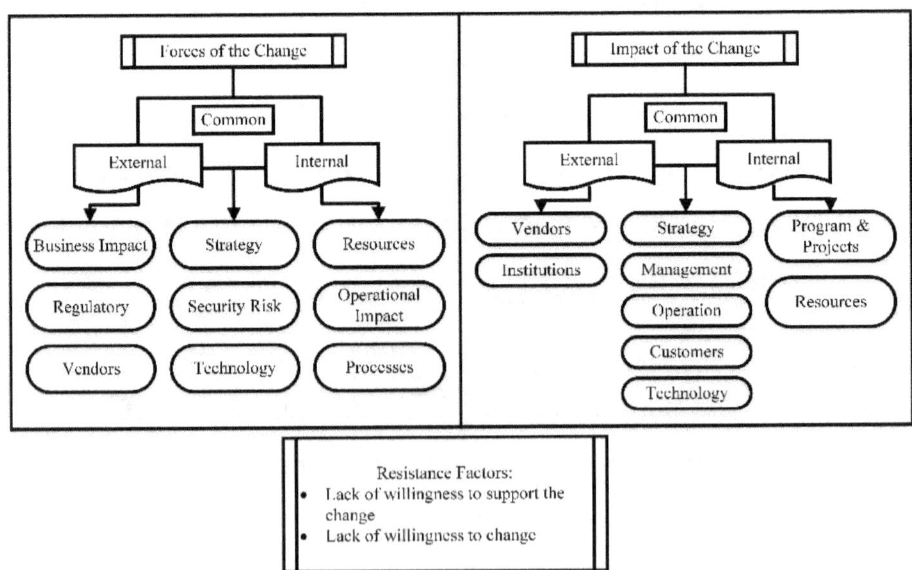

Figure 22 Description: Changes are inevitable. What is important here is to understand the signs and triggers of change, its impact on the organization and workforce, and, finally, what you can do to protect yourself.

You might wonder about the level of detail regarding a change in the IS/IT section and chapter. Well, most triggers for change start at the IS/IT pillar, even if the initial idea is

Figure 22 - - Alignment of Change Strategy

not from this pillar, and you can estimate the incoming impacts on employees. From the illustration above, you can also navigate the IS/IT strategy and policies to understand their functionality and the workspace they cover.

In general, here are the "Key Success Factors" (KSF) of an IS/IT pillar:

1. Understand the current industry, strategy, goals, objectives, and risks
2. Be in sync with the Information Technology industry, strategies, goals, objectives, and risks
3. Be and stay resilient and sustainable
4. Maintain a steady audit of the entire landscape for optimization, consolidation, innovation, or retirement. It is the definition of "Continuous Improvement".

Due to the disappearance of a single independent department or team, Quality Assurance and Audit, from the organizational structure, the vulnerability rate of any change failing has increased.

There would be an argument that the last paragraph is not valid or accurate. Countless programs and projects were completed and deployed to production without a QA department. The question is: what is the quality of that product or service? (The quality of a product or a service is the key element to validate the true need for a QA, which is a doable action by having a reliable audit without any bias or influence of involved stakeholders, to draw an impartial audit result. An example of such an audit is done by the "Baldrige Performance Excellence" Framework.

A failure should be measured against the entire organization, rather than a single project. i.e., when a single project or change fails, every allocated resource to that project would also be in a failed state, not just the so-called project team itself, but the business as well.

In the world of competition, there is a fine line between the number one and number two automakers, as well as between rankings and ratings. A single project failure could change the ranking overnight.

An organization's metrics over its audit must show the following to be number one:

- Efficiency
- Effectiveness
- Validity
- Reliability

All four ratings above are scientific measurements indicating that it is at the "Operational Excellence" layer or has a "High Performance" rating. The metrics must cover every pillar, not just one.

By simply stating a sentence, without presenting any quantitative and qualitative metrics and data that your organization possesses, that it is an "Operational Excellence" or is a "High Performance", no one with a knowledge of a true audit framework would accept that claim. Reminder that data collection and its targeted values are also key factors in the QA and Audit processes.

Indicating the number of employees with professional certifications and their educational levels, tactical abilities, without a strategic plan, is anything but an "Operational Excellence" or a "High Performance".

"Tactics without Strategy is nothing but failure."
(*The Art of War*, Sun Tzu)

There are many frameworks that an IS/IT utilizes for its operations, such as ITIL, Six Sigma, TQM, PMI, CMMI, etc. Without a valid and reliable audit, such as the Baldrige Performance Excellence framework, any operational metrics would be highly questionable.

Since 2008, after the great recession, when HRM evolved further toward a robust Human Resource procurement, organizations have leaned toward a faster closure of a change from enterprise-level programs or projects to simple operational updates or upgrades.

The goal is a short-term Net Profit, at the expense of efficiency and effectiveness. Presenting a change as an operational maintenance update is much faster and less costly than a project that requires more time and money to complete. The risk and impact of such a change is, at its core, a lack of proper planning, which will fail to deliver a sustainable product or a service.

There is an idealistic strategy in an IS/IT division called "Management by Science". This means:

- "Incorporating a reliable and valid process and procedures which would result in maximum efficiency and effectiveness in productivity, either in service or manufacturing industries, by lowering operational cost, while maintaining a healthy revenue with a reliable growth, in a competitive world."

There is a lot to think about in that single sentence above. Following up on the Sales and Marketing chapter, you would see the importance of the internet and its dominance in business today.

The Sales and Marketing objectives are directly connected to the IS/IT initiatives in terms of their risks and impacts. A product or service delivery time matters. This is where operational effectiveness comes into play. After that comes the efficiency calculations:

- Was the product delivered on time to the targeted consumer?
- Did the product satisfy the consumer's expectation?
- Was the operational cost less or higher than the sale price?
- Is that cost sustainable, or even better, could it be lowered?

The landscape of an IS/IT pillar is to keep operational costs lower than revenue, compared to competitors offering similar products and services.

What is the lowest cost in the scenario below:

In a major enterprise-wide systems update, support teams need to be available 24/7 to help customers with issues.

Scenario 1: IS/IT management hires additional support teams to be available for 6 months.

Scenario 2: IS/IT management engages all existing resources to work long hours to cover support needs.

How would the decision be affected in each of the following pay strategies:

- Support team is an hourly rate.
- The support team is salary-based.

You most likely would ask: What is the confidence level in doing the updates and upgrades with minimal risk and impact? Causing almost no problems.

This opens another line of questions over how a program would be managed and implemented. The faster the updates are completed, meaning less analysis, planning, and development time is spent, the sooner the systems will be delivered back to operations, if all goes well.

Many organizations are removing QA teams and leaving QA management to delivery managers, creating a conflict of interest right at the door.

You got the idea of what the results of the updates would look like and why support afterward is critical.

By adding the cost of program and project management to the required support, you can see how important it is to keep costs down to achieve the end-of-year net profit.

What or how would this affect your job or employment?

The working class will inevitably face job impacts, whether through mass layoffs, forced retirements, or other HRM and management practices. Still, there are safeguards one can follow to survive today's job market.

In Summary

The IS/IT department, pillar, or unit, has the largest budget in most organizations; therefore, a single pillar has the most impact on the job market, which ties back to your career path. It is given that technology is the way forward, but it is not written that you must work in the technology sector. There are other career paths within an IS/IT department. Program and project management is one branch in there, for which you do not have to be a programmer or a software engineer. Yet it would be an advantage to have some technological skills.

Some of the biggest organizational failures occurred in this pillar due to poor decision-making by CIOs or CTOs who were not closely monitoring the bits and bytes of the departments they were supposed to manage.

There are some major lessons learned out of this single department that today's workforce should pay very close attention to, especially when there is an incoming organizational change, such as Mergers & Acquisitions. That is the clue for what comes next.

Chapter 7: Integrated View

An integrated view is a consolidated view of all pillars. This would be a roadmap from the leadership seat to the last person in the operations team.

If you ever ponder the idea of having your own business, you could believe it. It is as simple as a plumber, an electrician, a doctor, a dentist, a lawyer, a yoga trainer, or a black-belt martial arts trainer who wants to be their own boss by opening their own business. The process is simply registering their business with the state registrar; for the State of Michigan, one would register with the "Department of Licensing and Regulatory Affairs". That is the easy part.

For a business or organization to survive, there are key elements that must be cared for so it can live long. Here are those initial vital keys:

1. Customers: a geographic area with people who can afford to buy your products and services.
2. Demands: among those possible customers, some of them are willing to buy your products and services.
3. Products and services: without this key element, you have no business.

Take any of the above key elements out of the list, and you have no possible business to conduct.

You might question item number two, the demands. You are right. There might not be a demand, and that is where a marketing strategy comes into play to create that demand. As a salesperson once said:

"People do not know what they want exactly; just show them something interesting. When you catch their eyes, you have a customer."

For now, let us pass that and stay with the basics.

These three critical elements are essential for an organization to survive.

For a village with 50 residents, a shoemaker would have no problem managing his business.

- What if the next village down the road has no shoemakers?
- What if the population increases to 100 people?
- What if another shoemaker shows up in the town and opens another shoe store?

The "what if" scenarios are what a business has to work with to survive.

Let us return to the overall landscape of today's global, interconnected economy, with consumers worldwide in mind. Every pillar you read about in previous chapters would have to consider the same three critical elements to keep the organization alive: collective support and collaboration.

What do you think some of the U.S. automotive companies did after a new car maker was born in 2003?

Moving to 2004, multiple automakers in the U.S. initiated massive changes around common elements, due to the following changes and events happening since a new automaker was born:

- Sales decline
- Production cuts
- Retiring some car models
- Introducing new brands

The mass layoff that followed was a matter of survival, at least from one perspective, to compete with the newly born automaker, a cost-cutting measure.

On the other side of the coin, in the same industry, one Japanese automaker made astonishing progress:

- Higher sales
- Hybrid revolution
- Expansion across the globe

These are the historical facts that have already made their way into textbooks and the online information highways. Just Google the major changes in the 2003 automotive industry due to the new entry.

What you would want to realize here is the contrast among these automakers. One of the German automakers was somewhere between these global rivals. The German automaker was in the same harsh landscape as its U.S. counterparts, but not close to the Japanese.

The point here is to understand how integrated the pillars are within an organization to save a company's livelihood.

Some takeaways from the above scenarios:

- Would the high salary package of the CEO matter when the question about mass layoffs comes to play?
- Was the management team's performance the cause of finding itself in a no-win situation, but proceeding with mass layoffs?

It is worth noting Toyota's management strategy and style.

- Adaptability
- Resiliency
- Efficiency and effectiveness

The above strategic policies are achievable through reliable and valid quality and audit controls and metrics. That is what has been lacking in many companies where the author worked.

While it is understandable that an organization would resort to mass layoffs or some downsizing strategy to save a company's existence, the critical questions remain unanswered:

- Could the company survive by adjusting just the C-Class pay packages, instead of mass layoffs?
- Could the company management teams, per pillars, reallocate resources to avoid mass layoffs?
- Could the company have a better internal audit to foresee the incoming financial or market troubles, and implement corrective actions to avoid mass layoffs?
- Is it possible, a hypothetical case, that an organization commences a mass layoff to preserve cash, under the name of cost-cutting and savings, for the year-end net profit report, so that the investors and shareholders would be satisfied?

The last bullet point is a very delicate strategy by an organization. A hypothesis needs to be proven with reliable data showing that some companies initiated an enterprise program after a mass layoff, once it is validated that the investment's cash value has been realized.

This goes back to the spaceship scenario in this book, how far a captain of a ship would go to decide what to save among the competing factors:

- The cargo
- The crew
- Or the whole ship

As a leader, a CEO, or a president, they have to make a tough decision, much like a spaceship captain. As far as the working class goes, employees should all plan for and be prepared for such scenarios ahead of their occurrence. Let us look at it more objectively.

- Would you rather be laid off, knowing that the company would survive, and other employees could still work? Or:
- Would you rather stay employed till the company goes bankrupt and closes its doors, having everyone lose their jobs, just because a mass layoff was avoided?

The first option should be a better choice, even though it is not a good choice for some.

These insights help the working class prepare to navigate changes or events within an organization that affect many employees, their jobs, and their livelihoods.

In Army training, there is a saying: "everyone pays for one's mistake." Unfortunately, it is not the same on the corporate planet. There are cases involving leadership and management mistakes that result in financial impact and necessitate cost-cutting measures, including mass layoffs, that affect the bottom layer of the workforce.

If you wonder why the keyword "mass layoff" keeps coming up, here is the reason. This phrase primarily refers to a set of strategies for HRM and management teams to use. These strategies have evolved over the past two decades, allowing the organization to reduce headcount without negative publicity or lawsuits.

This is why you need to be aware of strategies that will help you protect your job and your employment by proactively planning your exit and protecting your career.

From an integrative perspective, if all pillars are not in sync, a void will arise among them, negatively impacting leadership goals and objectives.

HRM Performance Tools could be a valuable strategy when used effectively with reliable, valid information, helping identify strengths and weaknesses, as well as options and threats to overall company goals.

An HRM tool used as a subjective strategy will negatively impact the workforce, affect performance and productivity, and result in low outcomes with high input, meaning a costly operation, lower net profit at the end of the fiscal year.

Lack of an independent Quality Audit is a major risk when HRM and management teams operate in isolation, away from the core organizational values and goals. The previous illustration of Strategic Operation would need one more pillar to complete an integrated need within an organization, that would be a "Quality and Audit" pillar, which would examine all pillars for their performance to make sure they are all aligned with the top vision and goals.

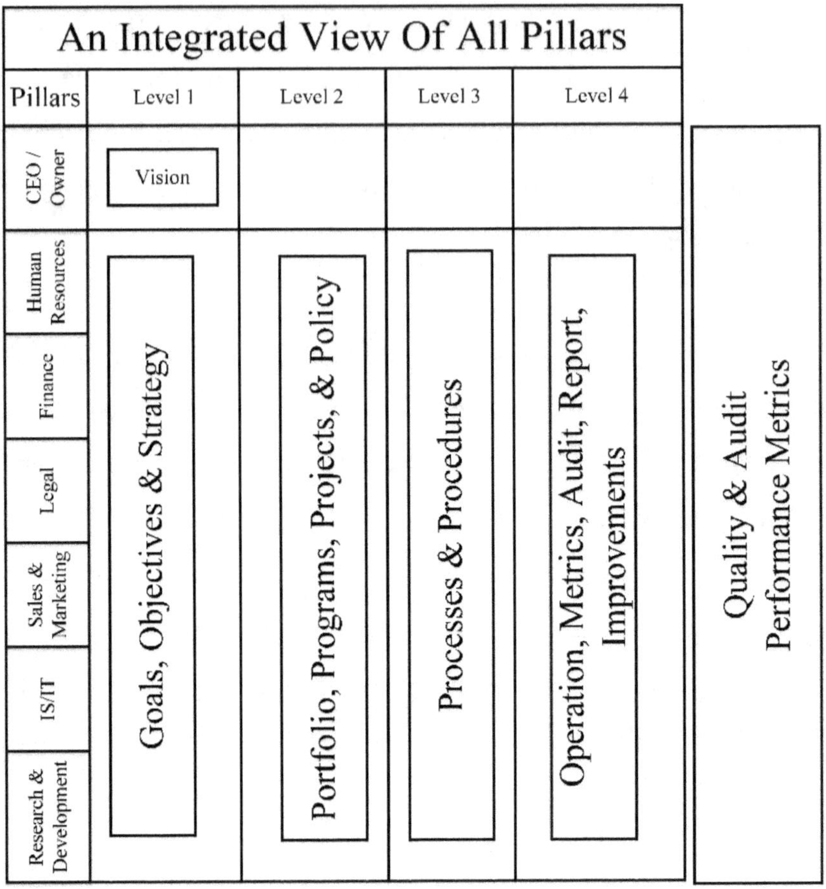

An Integrated View Of All Pillars					
Pillars	Level 1	Level 2	Level 3	Level 4	
CEO / Owner	Vision				
Human Resources	Goals, Objectives & Strategy	Portfolio, Programs, Projects, & Policy	Processes & Procedures	Operation, Metrics, Audit, Report, Improvements	Quality & Audit Performance Metrics
Finance					
Legal					
Sales & Marketing					
IS/IT					
Research & Development					

Figure 23- Integrated View

Figure 23 Description: Why aren't QA and Audit departments a stand-alone team or department, anymore? This is a critical question for the workforce to ask. One answer is: the results of independent QA and Audit would reveal the underlying impacts of a change on the organization, giving employees, the working class, the most powerful tool to recognize what is coming next, i.e., a mass layoff. To avoid such chaos in the workplace, the strategy, by design, is to remove an independent QA and Audit department.

Through a valid and reliable audit, an impending impact could be identified ahead of its inception, enabling corrective action on time. To highlight the above case about the Quality and Audit department:

At a town hall conducted by an executive member, a question was posed: Why isn't there a QA department?

The answer came fast: "Every pillar has its own QA within."

About a year later, the cost-cutting story came to light, leading to layoffs, and the reason was: "the organization needs to save operational costs to survive!"

Here is a short outline of what the purpose of a quality and audit department would look like:

1. Create a benchmark based on the strategic plan and the expected results.
2. Capture As-Is operational performance metrics, including the cost, the expenses, and the revenues.
3. Evaluate the benchmark with As-Is metrics to capture any gaps in the operation, in all pillars, based on each pillar's strategy and goals.

4. Conclude and summarize the evaluation to provide corrective actions to be taken, as needed, for re-aligning operational performance with the strategy and expected results.

That seems like a simple outline, yet the value of the above outline lies in an existential need to ensure a business stays in business before it hits the bottom line.

But let us say it here: having a Quality and Audit department is no guarantee if there is no influence or authority around it. Just getting the audit report does not mean a corrective action will follow.

There is a great opportunity for the HRM pillar to serve as the governance for the entire organization, using its own tool, the Performance Evaluation and Review system. But unfortunately, only a few are capitalizing on their HRM Strategy, while the majority are losing productivity and profitability daily.

The sad part is that the top layer lacks visibility into the lower management layer, making it difficult to make an independent assessment of goals and objectives, especially in global companies.

A hypothesis: A major impact at the middle management level could be seen in the misestimation of contingency costs for some operational events with no risk or impact, yet the cost would be the over-allocation of operational resources.

How does that work? A scenario would reveal how a management team charged the internal customers for a contingency cost while hiring more resources than needed. When the organization faced difficulties, the same team proposed a cost-saving measure for their department, creating a false impression that the department was efficient and effective.

The solution was simple: cut the contingency cost and lay off resources who should not have been there in the first place. The customer would think they are getting a discount, and the operational cost would go down as well, giving the impression of cost savings to leadership.

The middle manager takes a cost-saving action that pleases internal or external customers while pleasing leadership. No one would ever know or be able to see that unless there is a reliable audit.

Nonetheless, a mass layoff was followed, yet no connection was made to reveal the misrepresentation of the extra cost. This is due to the lack of an internal independent audit.

In the above hypothesis, there is a need for internal agreements among the multiple pillars: IS/IT, HRM, SM/RD, and Finance and Accounting.

Without a layer of audit, an organization would lose valuable intellectual assets, its human resources. An audit result would reveal the competency and capability of the management teams in terms of the outcomes of their deliverables and events, as well as their performance. But by establishing a BAD (Blame, Attack, Deny) strategy supported by HRM, the management team would be able to continue its work.

The importance of an integrated quality and audit department is to create transparency across all pillars, so that a big-picture view is always available to illustrate the individual pillar's strategy in action. Let us downsize this integrative space to one, removing the need for a PMO (Project Management Office).

If there is no PMO in an IS/IT department, you have a financial risk. This is not about the PMO team, but about having a strategy plan for managing the financial elements of that department, leaving a black hole visible only to that department head, not to anyone else in the organization.

If you see an HRM performance tool that is not showing any updates by management, but only your feedback, that is a black hole to mask the performance rating strategy, which is no strategy, yet a subjective method.

If your executives say something about what is going to happen, followed by your HRM giving another version of similar information, and finally, your own management team tells you to ignore the other ones, then you should be worried about what is going to happen, because there are two realities:

1. The leadership is confusing you to mask an incoming impact on your workplace.
2. The organization, from within, has no integration among its pillars, leaving you in the dark to find your career path.

By experiencing the past events, the 90s, 2000, 2008, 2019, and 2025, all had a mix of messages from both groups, but eventually HRM refined the strategy for mass layoffs, and one was far more evolved than the other, a learning over two decades.

The Research and Development (R&D) pillar, in connection with Sales and Marketing, is yet another valuable entity, with an impact on the workplace and the workforce at large. What R&D matters a lot, to the point of a serious financial setback. The only way to prevent creating or building something that will not generate revenue is to have clear Quality and Audit reports on its work.

Let us review an example whose failure brought chaos to the entire department.

A team of two engineers and an analyst was working on a software package for an internal client to minimize the client's effort to update a global database. While the development team was working on a solution and building it up, the client himself proceeded with his own research. Since there was no proper audit between the two groups, the effort of one team went to waste when the supporting client brought his own tool and cancelled the request for in-house development. Due to the cost-effectiveness of that endeavor, management had no choice but to remove the entire development team. Whose fault was that? Why did that happen?

At the end of the day, the client has the right to take the most efficient and effective path for his business. What was missed was clear quality and audit measurements to validate the development work and assess its value.

In the above case, a PMO team would have helped manage and control the development from the start.

Many enterprise programs followed the same fate as the case above, with a far more devastating cost impact. Again, the lack of an independent entity within an organization allowed such a loss. Can you guess who, in the end, paid the price and what the impact was on the workplace?

In Summary

This chapter provides a perspective on the importance of integrating all pillars within an organization. The only way to guarantee successful integration among these pillars is to have a valid and reliable transparency strategy, typically involving an audit.

A lack of top-down transparency would affect any job performance review and ratings. Without a valid and reliable audit demonstrating that a single task has achieved a targeted goal or strategy, there cannot be an accurate job performance rating.

In the era of interconnected social media, customers are more in touch with an event than ever. Whether customers will continue doing business depends heavily on their socio-economic behavior. For this reason alone, any organization in any industry should reassess its internal metrics for performance across each pillar to ensure they align with customers' socio-economic expectations.

Conclusion

At this time, you should have a general understanding of what an organizational landscape is, along with its pillars, and how the holistic operational strategy would impact your job, your employment, and your earnings.

Let us all agree:

- Without any employees, there cannot exist a business, unless you are self-employed
- Without a business, there is no employment for anyone, unless it is a one-person shop, self-employed.
- There exists a dependency between the entity and its employees, along with that comes an existential balance to be kept on both sides.

It is a symbiotic relationship. Unfortunately, in most cases, employers have more advantages than employees in hiring and termination.

As you learned, an organization is constantly on watch to do whatever it takes to survive, and that also applies to its employees, the working class. To make this field-level, the working class needs to be prepared for any sudden change that could result in job loss.

A change is inevitable; it will happen sooner or later. In parallel, you should not try to resist any change, and this is, by all means, a fact of the business. Instead, your effort should be focused on doing your best while preparing your skills and expertise for the impact of the change on your employment.

Learning and understanding the organizational pillars would help you navigate change much more easily and prepare you for the inevitable: an impact on employment.

Use your HRM systems to learn about your employer. The intranet would help you navigate the pillars and their associated structure and functions. Make an effort to learn and understand your employer. Only through that understanding could you prepare yourself for the worst-case scenario. Nevertheless, there is always an option, another opportunity outside of your current workplace. The fundamental question for the workforce is:

- Would the workforce do whatever it takes to get and keep the job? At what cost? And for how long?

There is always an employer with a task at hand, for which someone would be willing to do it. But that does not guarantee a fair market price and pay for the work.

- How low would you go in your expectations to get that job?

Postscript

You either "work to live" or "live to work". Only you could decide that.

Acknowledgments

This book series is a culmination of all the souls the author has encountered during his lifetime of working and learning. At each workplace, countless managers and employees were instrumental in the author's learning and experiences, good, bad, or ugly. Without them, writing this book series would not have been possible. Great thanks to all of them.

Here are some special workplaces that contributed a great deal to the author's learning and experiences:

- Source One Mortgage Service Company
- Kmart
- Accenture / DOW
- Ally Bank
- Fiat-Chrysler Automotive (FCA)
- Bank of America
- Mercedes-Benz

On the academic platform, each institution and university contributed a unique set of professors and instructors, who provided numerous insights that significantly shaped the contents. Their advice beyond the textbooks was the valuable learning the author gained at each workplace, which helped achieve a successful career. Great thanks to all of them.

- Oakland Community College
- Mott Community College
- Oakland University
- University of Michigan
- Dale Carnegie Course

There is one very special person in the author's life who has been standing by him throughout his career and helping him to withstand all the possible changes in the workplace, and that special person is his wife, Karen.

About the author

James Ostad is a diverse writer for diverse audiences. One of his writing genres is in the business and employment landscape.

He has worked across several industries, spanning global markets. Some of the major industries are Finance, Education, Healthcare, Automotive, Retail, and Manufacturing.

James obtained his education in Michigan, with an Associate degree in Business Management, a bachelor's degree in Computer Science, and a master's degree in Business Administration (AAS, BS, MBA).

He also achieved professional certificates and training, the highlights are:

- Dale Carnegie Course,
- Baldrige Performance Examiner,
- ITIL,
- PMP-PMI,
- CISSP-TC.

In his writings, James draws on his lifelong experiences, including his professional work, travel across three continents, his professional training and education, and sports.

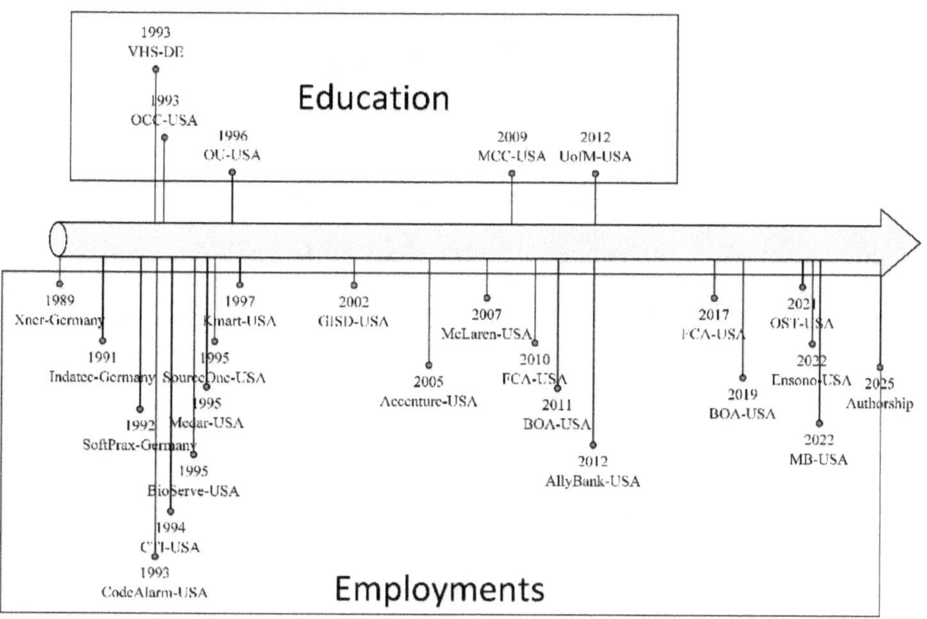

Figure 24 - Author's Professional

You can contact the author at james@ostads.com with your comments and questions.

For a complete professional profile, visit https://www.linkedin.com/in/jamesostad/.

Copyright permissions

All contents of this book are from the author's personal knowledge, his working experiences, and his education. Any references from books or articles have been noted in the bibliography for credit, as well as those in public records.

Discussion questions

After reading this volume of this book series, you might want to explore further reading, around the following questions:

At the personal level -

- What does a job performance and its rating mean in a workplace?
- What does a job description vs. a job title mean by HRM?
- How far would you go to keep a job?
- What would you do to improve your hiring prospects and secure your working career?

At the professional level –

- What are the best characteristics of a manager?
- What are the worst characteristics of a manager?
- How would you deal with a toxic manager?
- How would you deal with a toxic HRM?

Appendix

This is the first edition of this book series, which will have three volumes, with this one being the first.

The next two volumes are written based on the contents of this volume. Therefore, it is highly recommended to read the first volume before proceeding to the next volumes.

Figures and Tables

Figures

Tables

Index

Bibliography

This bibliography includes some of the major books from the author's lifetime at work that had a great influence on his learning and experiences. This book was put together from those learning experiences.

Miller, Roger LeRoy; Jentz, Gaylord A. **Fundamentals of Business Law**: Summarized Cases, 8th Edition 2010, Thomson South-Western, Cengage Advantage, Ohio, USA."

Schermerhorn, John R.JR. **Management**, 9th Edition 2008, John Wiley & Sons, New Jersey, USA

Longenecker, Justin G.; Moore, Carlos W.; Petty, J. William; Palich, Leslie E. **Small Business Management** 2008, Thomson South-Western, Cengage Learning, Ohio, USA

Greer, Charles R.; Plunkett, W. Richard **Supervisory Management**, 11th Edition, 2007, Pearson Prentice Hall, New Jersey, USA

Sloane, Arthur A.; Witney, Fred **Work Relations**, 12th Edition, 2007, Pearson Prentice Hall, New Jersey, USA

Dessler, Gary **Human Resources Management**, 11th Edition 2008, Pearson Prentice Hall, New Jersey, USA

Thompson, Leigh L. **The Mind and Heart of the Negotiator**, 5th Edition, 2012, Pearson Prentice Hall, New Jersey, USA

"Anderson, David R.; Sweeney, Dennis J.; Williams, Thomas A.; Camm, Jeffrey D.;

Martin, Kipp. **An Introduction to Management Science**, 13th Edition, 2011, South-Western Cengage Learning, Ohio, USA.

Baldwin, Timothy T.; Bommer, William H.; Rubin, Robert S. **Developing Management Skills**: What Great Managers Know and Do. 1st edition 2008, McGraw-Hill Irwin, New York, USA

Baron, James N.; Kreps, David M. **Strategic Human Resources**: Frameworks for General Managers, 1999, John Wiley & Sons, New Jersey, USA

Baron, David P. **Business and Its Environment**, 7th Edition, 2013, Pearson Prentice Hall, New Jersey, USA

Jacobs, F. Robert; Chase, Richard B. **Operations and Supply Chain Management**, The Core, 3rd Edition, 2013, McGraw-Hill Irwin, New York, USA

Hill, Charles **International Business**, 9th Edition, 2012, McGraw-Hill Irwin, New York, USA

Peng, Mike W. **Global Strategy**, 3rd Edition, 2014, South-Western Cengage Learning, Ohio, USA

David, Fred R.; David, Forest R. **Strategic Management, Concepts and Cases**, 5th Edition 2015, Pearson Prentice Hall, New Jersey, USA

Boone, Louise E.; Kurtz, David L. **Contemporary Business**, 11th Edition, 2008, Thomson Custom Solution, Mason, OH, USA

Brealey, Richard A.; Myers, Stewart L.; Allen, Franklin; **Principles of Corporate Finance**, 10th edition; 2011, McGraw-Hill Irwin, New York, USA

Horngren, Charles T.; Harrison, Walter T.; Oliver, M. Suzanne; **Accounting 8e**; 2009, McGraw-Hill Irwin, New York, USA

Weygandt, Jerry J.; Kieso, Donald E.; Kimmel, Paul D.; **Principles of Financial Accounting**; 2007, 8th edition, John Wiley & Sons, New Jersey, USA

References

Covey, Stephen R., **Principle Centered Leadership**, 1990, Simon & Schuster, New York, USA

Ury, William, **Getting Past No**, 1991, Bantam Dell, New York, USA

Ury, William; Fisher, Roger, **Getting to Yes**, 1981, Penguin Group, New York, USA

Musashi, Miyamoto, **The Book of Five Rings**, 1982, Bantam Books, New York, USA

Sun Tzu, The Art of War, Public Domain

ITIL, Information Technology Infrastructure Library, https://en.wikipedia.org/wiki/ITIL

Six-Sigma, https://en.wikipedia.org/wiki/Six_Sigma

TQM, Total Quality Management, https://en.wikipedia.org/wiki/Total_quality_management

Baldrige Performance Excellence Framework, https://www.nist.gov/baldrige/publications/baldrige-excellence-framework

CMMI, **Capability Maturity Model Integration** https://en.wikipedia.org/wiki/Capability_Maturity_Model_Integration

Major Professional Training's impact on creating this book:

1996 Time Quest, Franklin Quest Co., MI, USA

2004 How to Become a Better Communicator, SkillPath, MI, USA

2004 How to Balance Priorities & Manage Multiple Projects, Fred Pryor, MI, USA

2004 Dale Carnegie Course, MI, USA

2005 Leader's Window, Charter Oak Consulting Group Inc., MI, USA

2007 Project Management Professional,

2007 Competencies for Tomorrow's Managers, SkillSoft Co., MI, USA

2007 Career Counselor Essentials, SkillSoft Co., MI, USA

2007 Designing a Job Description Incorporating Job Competencies, SkillSoft Co., MI, USA

2007 Creativity and Innovation, SkillSoft Co., MI, USA

2009 How to Write a Business Plan, SBA.Gov, USA

2017 Crucial Conversation, ASU, AZ, USA

The Author's Work History

Accenture, Michigan, USA

Ally Bank, Michigan, USA

Bank of America, Michigan, USA

Bio-Serv-Corporation, Michigan, USA

Code Alarm, Michigan, USA

Concept Technology Inc., Michigan, USA

Dow Chemical, Michigan, USA

Dynamic People, Michigan, USA

EDS, Michigan, USA

Ensono, Michigan, USA

Express Personnel Services, Michigan, USA

Fiat Chrysler Automotive, Michigan, USA

Genesee Intermediate School Districts, Michigan, USA

Genesis 10, Michigan, USA

Indatec GmbH, Bayern, Germany

Infomatics Inc., Michigan, USA

Kmart, Michigan, USA

McLaren, Michigan, USA

Medar, Michigan, USA

Mercedes-Benz Financial Services, Baden-Württemberg / Michigan, Germany / USA

Open System Technology (OST), USA, Michigan, USA

PHNS, Michigan, USA

Robert Half Technology, Michigan, USA

Security Inspection Inc., Michigan, USA

SoftPrax GmbH, Bayern, Germany

Source One Mortgage Services, Michigan, USA

Strategic Staffing Solution, Michigan, USA

TaskPro IT, Michigan, USA

TTI USA, Michigan, USA

University of Michigan, Michigan, USA

V2Soft, Michigan, USA

Western Temporary Services, Michigan, USA

Xner GmbH, Bayern, Germany

Book volumes in this edition

Workplace, Unwritten Policies, Academic vs Experiential Views:

- Volume **one**: Basic Organizational Structure - an introduction to the general and basic structure of an organization, with limited comments and a sample of workplace events. The intention is to give readers a perspective on the big picture of the workplace in relation to their employment.
- Volume **two**: Organizational Changes and Events – a series of situational cases related to the actual workplace events and changes, with a systematic introduction of the case. The intent is to provide a strategic and behavioral view of those events so that an individual employee can recognize the impact on the workforce and on the individual's employment.
- Volume **three**: Strategies for Workforce, Employees – a comprehensive list of strategies and best practices at the workplace for any employees, with any skill set, in any industry, and in any geographical location. Empowering any employees to be able to:
  - Learn the environment they work in
  - Understand their job expectations and requirements
  - Recognize a change or an event for its triggers that would bring an impact or risk to an employee's employment status.
  - Strategies and plans for protecting their employment and career, be proactive and engaged at work, while planning for a sudden exit, at will, or by force.

Afterward

The author's intention in writing this book has always been clear: to answer those questions for which he himself did not have the answers when he needed them the most.

Here are some of those questions:

Big Picture

- How would I know if the company is going to lay off our team?
- How do I plan in an ever-changing job market for a career path that would be sustainable?
- Why was I let go when all I was doing was my assigned job?
- Why did HRM not respond to my complaint?
- Why did my salary agreement change after I was hired?
- How would I know if, during the layoffs, I would be getting any final paycheck?

Department Level

- Why does my manager behave that way?
- What shall I do if my manager threatens my job if I do not do what s/he asks me?
- What should I do when my manager yells at me or insults me?
- Why are my tasks being taken away by my manager?

Personal Level

- How would I explain my last job separation to the next employer?
- What should I do when I am fired without cause?
- Where would I get some directions?
- What can I do to secure my employment at my workplace?
- How would I plan for a sudden termination?

Anecdotes

While working 60 hours per week in the factory, I was going to school half-time and living paycheck to paycheck on minimum wage. I got to a point where I realized I was being paid less than those hired after me for doing the same work.

I decided to gather my courage and ask the supervisor for a raise. When I asked the supervisor, I explained the cost of my school and living situation. She looked at me, burst into laughter, and turned around to walk away.

That job was my livelihood at a young age, and I had no support.

I did the same thing that day. I quit. The temporary agency called me to ask why I was not at work. I explained that to him, but he got mad and demanded that I go back immediately.

The next day, I went to the temporary agency to pick up my final check. The agency manager called me into his office and started yelling at me. After he was finished, I asked him: "May I have my last check, please?

He replied, “Get out, go get it from the secretary, it’s at her desk.”

It was hard to leave the job I depended on, with no other job waiting to start. But it felt good to stand up for myself.

My lesson learned list:

- I can do it too, but with a strategy and planning.
- Know my values, soft and hard skills.
- Take action, proactively, and consider delayed gratification.
- Be Smart, never stop learning.
- Always be calm, stay with facts.
- Do your best, with proficiency.
- Don’t steal, don’t lie, be honest.

Build yours.

www.ingramcontent.com/pod-product-compliance
Lightning Source LLC
LaVergne TN
LVHW010617100826
845148LV00014B/2999

* 9 7 8 1 7 3 5 2 0 5 9 2 2 *